60 CENTS

SECRETS AND TALES
IN A SMALL TOWN

BRAD HULSEY

Library of Congress Control Number: 2016941485

ISBN: 978-1-943529-52-0 paperback
       978-1-943529-53-7 eBook

Printed in the United States

Front cover photo of well by Brad Hulsey
Rear cover photo by Buell Hulsey

For more information, visit **www.60cents.net**

To my dear children, Joseph, Evan and Lane. You make me proud each and every day. Always remember your heritage, and never forget to help someone in need.

May you always be blessed. I love you!

ACKNOWLEDGEMENTS

There are so many persons I could thank for helping me to become an author of this book. I could never name you all, but I do appreciate you immensely. First and foremost, I am eternally grateful to my wife, my partner, my soulmate and my best friend, Tracy. Sweetheart, I couldn't have accomplished this without your love, support and encouragement. I love you – infinity-plus, Trace!

My brother, Phil, has been a great encourager and supporter of me throughout the process of my writing this book. Phil, you are the best brother a guy can have. Thank you for all you have done for me. I love you, Brother!

To my dear family and friends who have helped me in my research and who have encouraged, inspired and supported me, I thank you all, namely: Doris (Aunt Dossie) Hardy; my first cousin, Julia Woods Beck; Johnny Pannell; Greg Gray; the City of Rockmart; Rockmart Historical Museum; Polk County Superior Court Clerk's office; Rockmart Civic Arts Commission; Reverend Lavay McCullough and family; Babe Atkins-Byrne; Randy and Susan Hardy; Cathy Matthews; Margaret Bennett Jacobs; Lucy Harris Cromer; Jeff Ellis; Stacey Smith; Leigh Hulsey; Cynthia Lanning; Anna Zikmundová; and, my wonderful in-laws, Jim and Jane Sirmans, Greg Sirmans and Ernest and Kathy Moreland.

TABLE OF CONTENTS

CHAPTER ONE: SOUTHERN BOYHOOD

In a small town, everyone usually knows the details of everybody else's business. Even closely guarded secrets can't remain hidden for long, unless the person who is the steward of the secret is dead (or even worse). How, then, could the truth have been hidden from this small town boy for more than twenty-five years?

Looking back, I guess I must have been oblivious to an ominous truth that I didn't have a clue even existed. I feel like I was a victim of circumstance...or should I say I was a victim of circumstantial evidence? Others in town knew all along about the secret that would eventually rock my world. I guess I was viewed as the hometown boy turned into a man who was on a need-to-know basis and, you know what they say – I didn't need to know.

It isn't "what" happened that now haunts me, but instead it's the secret that was kept from me for oh so many years that wounds me to my core. To be honest – really, really honest – what bothers me more than anything is that the steward of the secret was the one who was supposed to be my protector, the one whom I most trusted, most admired and most loved – right up there with Momma.

How could my own father have kept it all from me? I could have accepted this revelation much more easily if it had been veiled from me only by other family or friends. But for my own father, my flesh and blood, to have kept a story this big tucked away in his memory bank for all those years – seriously? I have a story to tell – yes. I am emotional – yes. Who wouldn't be? It all took place in the same small town.

****

During his senior year at Rockmart High School in Rockmart, Georgia, my father was nominated by Georgia's Junior United States Senator Richard B. Russell, to attend the U.S. Military Academy at West Point, New York. Senator Russell was a former Governor of Georgia, and he had a compelling reason to nominate Daddy (as I affectionately called my father) for this high honor. Daddy always liked to tell the story of how Senator Russell wanted so badly for him to become a cadet and to succeed at West Point.

What Daddy never told was why the good Senator wanted so desperately for him to accept his nomination. This wouldn't be revealed to me until many years after Daddy's death. Instead of taking advantage of that fine education, Daddy decided that he didn't want to leave Momma (my dear, sweet mother) behind, and the U.S. Military decided they needed him in a different position, drafting him during World War II into the U.S. Marines.

Having eloped to Center, Alabama with a couple of friends on hand as witnesses, my mother and father were married on Christmas Day of 1942. They would set up their first home on First Avenue in the Goodyear Village in Rockmart.

After being drafted into the Marine Corps in 1943, Daddy left to serve our country, staying stateside during World War II.

While Daddy was away at the Marine base at Camp Lejeune, North Carolina, Momma spent her time working at the local Goodyear Mill. She enjoyed her friends and the company of her grandmother, Fannie "Ma" Williams, who would come to visit from time-to-time from her home in Dallas, Georgia. Ma Williams was a fixture in Dallas and Paulding County, having served as a midwife and assisting with the birth of most of the babies in the area back in the 1920s through the 1940s.

Daddy would return home from Camp Lejeune after only one year. Having suffered multiple hernias and subsequent surgeries, he was dismissed on a Medical Honorable Discharge, never having to go to war. He went back home to Rockmart, to his new bride, and to begin a new life for himself and his family.

Daddy needed someone to help him understand and cope with being a husband, providing for a family, paying bills, maintaining a house – all of those things that a responsible man has to deal with on a daily basis. He needed his own father, but my grandfather couldn't be there for him. It was impossible.

Momma and Daddy tried for years to have children. On July 27, 1958, their firstborn came into the world, my older brother, Phillip Edward Hulsey, affectionately known as Phil. Three years, three months and one day later (Phil and

60 CENTS

I always liked citing the exact time between our births), after having a miscarriage between the birth of Phil and me, I was born to Fred Avery Hulsey, Jr. and Martha Holland Hulsey on October 28, 1961. Welcome to the family, Brad Alan Hulsey. Dr. Charlie Smith, for whom Momma later worked for many years, delivered me that day at 6:44 p.m. in the Rockmart-Aragon Hospital.

While it was a small facility, Rockmart took great pride in having its own local hospital. I take great pride in having been born there. Momma said that delivering me hurt so badly, she actually threatened to kill the nurse assisting Dr. Smith that day. I think I must have nearly killed her coming out! I later learned that Momma and Daddy had decided to only have two children maximum and that, had she not have miscarried the second child, I never would have been conceived and born.

My maternal grandparents, "Shad" and Jo Ellen Holland, whom Phil and I affectionately called "Poppy" and "Maw Maw" Holland, were on hand for my birth, as well as my paternal grandmother, Verdie Mae Hulsey Weaver, whom we lovingly called "Maw Maw" Vert. I wish my paternal grandfather, Granddaddy Hulsey, could have been present. I'm sure Daddy wished that his father could have been there to greet his newborn baby grandson.

Two days after my birth, Momma, Daddy and Phil took me to our home on Goodyear Avenue, located in the Goodyear Village across from the Goodyear Tire and Rubber Company Mill. Two months later, we would move to a larger brick home on Ivy Street that had a roof constructed with slate from the old Rockmart quarry, first built and occupied by Sam D. Lee and his wife.

****

My dear family, from l to r: Fred Hulsey (Daddy); Phil Hulsey (brother); Martha Hulsey (Momma); me (I already look mischievous at that young age)

Growing up in Rockmart, Georgia was an experience that any red-blooded southern boy with an ounce of ingenuity would relish. Nestled in the foothills of the Northwest Georgia Mountains, a 50-mile one-way ride to Atlanta, Rockmart offered an abundance of small-town charm and a sense of community that many of the neighboring cities could only wish for. It was a place where everyone knew his neighbor's name, his lot in life and, yes, everybody's business. Founded in 1872, the Rockmart area was known primarily for its slate and rock quarries, which provided employment for many over the years, including Welsh settlers who had found their way into the area in 1838.

My buddies and I didn't have a single care in the world as we plotted our daily agendas filled with fun, fellowship and mischief. It didn't matter to us if we were at school, in our immediate neighborhood there on Ivy Street in Rockmart, or running around the entirety of the town. We were determined to have our own brand of recreation, no matter what. I've been told I inherited some of my mischievous ways from my Granddaddy Hulsey. Perhaps so but, unfortunately, I never had the opportunity to meet him.

Rockmart had been served by two major railroads years before I knew the difference between a Tyco Train Set and a surefire railway. On one of the railroads, both passenger and freight lines used to chug up and down the rails, transporting passengers from Atlanta via Rockmart all the way to Birmingham, Alabama. Going in to Rockmart, near the community of Van Wert and the old Hulsey farm place owned by Great-Granddaddy Hulsey, that particular rail line ran directly past Coots Lake and the upper lake just above.

These spots were two of my Granddaddy and Great-Granddaddy Hulsey's favorite fishing holes and homebrew drinking hideaways just outside of town. Once the rail line got into Rockmart, there was a spur line that ran directly into and through downtown Rockmart in a northeasterly direction toward Cartersville, Georgia.

Having dual rail systems running through the same town

made for economic opportunity. Rockmart is primarily an industrial city. During the 1960s and 1970s, the Goodyear Mill, Marquette Cement Plant, Galite Aggregate Plant and J.L. Lester & Son Wholesale Grocers provided much of the employment for the community. Each of these businesses was served by one or both of the rail systems.

Daddy worked at the Goodyear Mill most of his adult life, taking medical disability due to cancer after forty-one years of service. Momma worked at the same mill and at the Atlanta Gas Light Company local office for a few years before eventually going to work for Dr. Charlie Smith.

Later on in the 1980s and 1990s, I was in sales, advertising and sales management at J.L. Lester & Son. For thirteen-plus years there, I had the fortune of learning from accomplished business people like Raymond Lester, Jimmy Lester, Mary "Tiny" Simon, Jack Williams, Buren Thompson and Charles Hagan and Wayne Coalson, to name a few. Their guidance and instruction helped me to hone my business skills that would benefit me for the rest of my life.

****

Since its founding in 1898, the Goodyear Tire and Rubber Company has primarily been known for its high-quality tires and the iconic Goodyear Blimp. The Goodyear Mill, opened in Rockmart in 1929, provided the bulk of the jobs for area residents. It also brought on the largest influx of new residential construction and increased population in Rockmart history.

60 CENTS

My brother, Phil, and I got to fly on the blimp when we were young boys, courtesy of Daddy's generosity in letting us experience that joy instead of him doing it. He had a choice, and he chose us. What a thrill!

Rockmart's Goodyear wasn't a tire manufacturing plant. Its primary purpose was to fill defense contracts for rubberized fuel tanks and other armed forces-related rubberized products. The mill was most famously known, however, for being the Goodyear plant that manufactured and stored the large helium balloons that were proudly marched through the streets of New York City each Thanksgiving Day during the Macy's Thanksgiving Day Parade.

As boys, Phil and I got to join other children of Goodyear employees during the Christmas season for a celebration at the Goodyear Clubhouse, located at the Goodyear Golf Course adjacent to the Mill. We got to sit on Santa's lap, pick a gift of our own liking, and receive a stocking full of candy and fruit. There were usually two or three of the Macy's balloons inflated for our wonderment and delight. I can remember gazing with excitement at Superman, Bullwinkle, Underdog, Mickey Mouse, Popeye, Linus the Lion, Weeble, and Kermit the Frog, to name a few. They would be anchored and displayed nearby at the ninth hole of the golf course.

As I walked away with my Christmas stash and lifetime memories of the tinsel, garland, and the vibrant reds and greens that colored the landscape of that Christmas wonderland, little did I know what I would find many years later in that very same location. I had no idea that my childhood innocence in that very place and moment would one day become the starting point of a mystery that I never knew existed and would be unlocked.

Goodyear Mill – Rockmart, Georgia (Photo courtesy of Goodyear Tire & Rubber Company)

Goodyear Children's Christmas Party. That's me on Santa's lap. Phil is patiently waiting his turn.

Mickey Mouse, one of the balloons made at Goodyear Mill in Rockmart (Photo courtesy of the Rockmart Historical Museum)

Growing up, our weekends were usually filled with sports activities, attending Sunday School at the Rockmart First Baptist Church, the occasional shopping trip to Rome, Georgia (and a hamburger and French fries at McDonald's), a trip to downtown Rockmart to the "fountain" (the cafe at City Drug Store) and, my favorite of all — Momma's delicious, home-cooked Sunday dinner.

Back then you had lunch at midday during the weekdays and on Saturdays, but the big, after-Sunday School meal was called "dinner". Most Sundays, our family didn't attend the 11 a.m. worship service after Sunday School because we all couldn't wait to get home, change clothes, and dig in into Momma's culinary delights.

Every night, we would eat "supper". Momma was the best cook ever, hands down! I particularly loved when she would bake a ham or a beef or pork roast, and not just because I really enjoyed the taste. The aroma of the succulent meat would cover the house with its luscious, pungent fragrance that would last for weeks. One could savor the odor as he moved throughout the house.

Frying okra, green tomatoes or pork chops would provide another long-lasting delectable scent that would satisfy the senses for days to come. Eating them wasn't half-bad, either.

On one particular winter's Sunday morning, I pleaded with Momma and Daddy to let me stay for the worship service after Sunday School. A scattering of my buddies and I had secretly connived a plan to make faces at the pastor and choir from the front seat of the church's balcony. Of course, I didn't tell my parents that was why I wanted to stay.

My reasoning to them was of a "celestial" nature; I wanted to learn more about God. They fell for my ruse, and allowed me to stay for worship with my band of brothers. Daddy told me to meet him out front of the church as soon as worship was over.

My pals and I had a whale of a time during the service, looking down from on high in the balcony with some of the silliest and most distorted faces a young chap could conceive of. We were continually reprimanded by some of the adults who sat nearby, but that didn't stop us from continuing with our folly.

During the service, there was a time for the offering to be taken. The ushers passed the offering plates from one end of the pews to another on the main floor of the church's sanctuary. On that particular Sunday, there was no usher in the balcony. Daddy had given me a dime for me to give as my personal offering.

As I looked around for the usher in the balcony, and seeing that there was none, I had the smartest of ideas. I would drop my dime from the balcony down into the offering plate below once the usher on the main floor passed by underneath us. When the unsuspecting usher neared the pew closest for me to drop my ten cent offering, I whispered down to him, "Pssst...pssst. Hey, sir...catch!" Sending the dime into a tailspin as it fell from my grip downward, the usher quickly moved back and forth underneath me to position himself and the offering plate in just the right spot.

Suddenly, there was a loud "CLANG" that reverberated throughout the church as my offering landed squarely into the plate. As nearly every pair of eyes in the sanctuary glared at me, and with my chums giggling and snorting out of control, I gave the OK sign and loudly whispered to the dumbfounded usher, "Great catch!".

By then, another of the ushers had ascended into the balcony, and he swiftly escorted me down the stairs, through the vestibule of the church, and eventually stopped at the church office. He then proceeded to phone Daddy and informed him of my misbehavior.

Daddy rushed to the church, found me and the usher awaiting his arrival near the back of the Sunday School building, exited his still-running Plymouth Belvedere and wore my rear end out right there in front of God, the usher, and my snickering comrades who had followed us and hidden themselves behind the large air conditioning coolant system so that they could view my demise. For years after that, Momma and Daddy wouldn't let me attend worship services by myself. I guess I can see why.

****

At the City Drug Store fountain, Daddy would always get a cup of coffee, and Phil and I would each have a fountain-poured cola. In those days, a fountain drink was a treat. We didn't get anything to eat usually, but the memories of the sizzling hamburgers, steaming hot dogs and spicy chili still stir my taste buds to this day. There were two men who always happened to show up at the very same time that we would make our entrance at City Drug. One of them was, as I recall, small in stature and always appeared unshaven and somewhat disheveled.

In my youthful mind, this man reminded me of the infamous Emmett Kelly, who created and portrayed the clown "Weary Willie" for several years that depicted the hobos of the Great Depression era. He had been a local high school football hero in years gone by, just like Daddy had been in the 1930s and early 1940s, and had a name no one could forget.

The other fellow reminded me of the actor and comedian W.C. Fields. With his bright red nose and bloodshot eyes, this dapper gentleman always dressed perfectly, wearing a stylish fedora hat, and walking a wee bit gingerly with a cane.

Those two fellows were always so nice to Phil and me, and they always had a kind word or two for Daddy. Each man would sit on a stool at the counter of the fountain, and they would be served a cup of piping hot black coffee and what I termed as "water with bubbles popping all over the place". I would learn later that both of those fellows were actually a couple of the "town drunks", and their purpose at the City Drug fountain was for soothing their hangovers from their over-consumption the night before.

The water with bubbles was seltzer water with a Goody's Powder mixed in to assist with the headache brought on from the prior night's indulgence. I, also, learned much later that they had played a key protective role in the upbringing and maturation of Daddy.

****

As young boys, especially growing up in a small town, we often used our imaginations to create excitement in our lives and, sometimes, in other's lives, too. At the Marble Street railway crossing in Rockmart, there has existed for many-a-year a switchbox that contains the electronic mechanisms that, for one, controlled the warning lights at the intersection. It was (and still is) painted a shiny metallic silver hue, and it appeared to stand two heads taller than all of us little whippersnappers.

At that time, there were no crossing arms to hold back vehicles or pedestrians. On some evenings, just for kicks and giggles, my buddies and I would take a portable spotlight and an old air horn down to the switchbox. As we were hiding behind the silver monstrosity, we would wait expectantly for an unknowing vehicle to pass over the railroad crossing and then...BOOM...one of us would throw the switch on the spotlight; and then......BWAAAH-BWAAAH-BWAAH...another of us would sound the old air horn; and then...SCREEEEEEEECH...the vehicle's driver would maneuver his or her way all around that rail crossing in order not to be massacred by the supposed and imagined oncoming, barreling-down-the-tracks train engine.

To say we got called every foul name in the book by unsuspecting and angry drivers and passengers would be an understatement. I can't remember anyone getting hurt from that form of mischief; except the time Daddy found out what we had been up to, and he blistered my behind with his size 32 belt. The days of the spotlight and old air horn had come to an end. Later, Daddy would share a confidential laugh with me, hidden from Momma's anger with me and my mischief. There were secrets of his own that Daddy would never share with me – secrets that I don't believe would have made him, or anyone else for that matter, laugh.

Aside from the spotlight and air horn shenanigans my friends and I would engage in around the railroad tracks, we devised and carried out other rascally activities, all in the name of fun. There was the simplest of them all – placing pennies on the railroad tracks, and when a train would barrel down the rails at top speed, running over the one-cent pieces, the coin would be stretched out beyond recognition. We used these for good luck charms afterward, along with four-leaf clovers we would find and pocket in the field next to the tracks. Momma washed many a clover in my pants pockets over the years.

A little more courageous and outrageous stunt was hopping on the train cars as they slowly crept down the tracks through town. One of the railroad company's trains blew through town like a frightened rabbit at a rapid pace. The other trains that ran along the spur to and from Cartersville, however, resembled an old, crusty turtle, slowly making its way down a straight and lonely path, or an old, tattered wagon being pulled by a worn-out mule.

The railway spur toward Cartersville ran parallel to Rockmart's main body of water and drinking water source, the Euharlee Creek. There is a very short overpass, in both width and height, in a hidden area near the creek that the slow-moving trains would pass over.

During the summertime, my partners-in-mischief and I would hop on the ladder of a railcar on the slow moving train near town, and when we came upon the overpass, we would hoist our bodies in a mighty leap off of the railcar and plunge with a mighty splash into the old swimming hole, located in the Euharlee Creek behind Findley Wiggins machine shop on North Marble Street. Every now and then, one of us would lose our courage, and that made for a weary trip down the tracks until we could find soft ground to hurl ourselves onto.

The ground was not as shock-absorbent as the waters of the Euharlee. But you were alright with the buddies if you had to take the ground action. Even though you were a fraidy cat about jumping off into the swimming hole, you didn't lose your man card when we all saw the poor soul rolling around on the ground in pain and agony. Usually, when we detected only a small amount of blood and sensed no broken appendages, we would leave the poor soul writhing and return to our splash fest in the cool waters of the Euharlee.

On one occasion, I, along with one of my Rockmart buddies and Little League baseball teammates, Butch Compton, hopped the slow-moving train in hopes of making a clean dive into the creek. Suddenly, the train began to pick up speed, far exceeding any that we had experienced before. We screamed to each other in fear, and in hopes that the train engineer or conductor would hear us, but to no avail.

Butch hollered to me that we had to jump and roll. I bellowed back at him that it was too risky, and that I wasn't about to jump. We both climbed into the open railcars for what wasn't a joy ride. We were on our way to Cartersville, Georgia and, what I assumed would be a butt whooping at best from Daddy and, at worst, a warrant for our arrests and a date in juvenile court. That is, if we made it to our final destiny alive.

Once the train stopped in Cartersville, Butch and I jumped off the train, and in full sight of the rapidly approaching conductor. Before he could say much, Butch and I confessed our transgressions, and pleaded for leniency. The conductor heard our pleas and proceeded to chew us out for our stupidity. He promised not to report what we had done to railway authorities, as long as Butch and I promised not to ever "jump" a train again. Of course, we immediately obliged the kind conductor with our promises.

Next, and least pleasant on our agendas, was to contact our parents. The conductor allowed us to use a phone in the station. It was a long distance call from Cartersville to Rockmart in those days, so I had to make a collect call to Momma and Daddy. I hoped Momma would answer the phone. My hopes were dashed as Daddy picked up the phone. I was mortified at hearing his voice. Once I told him my story, and I did tell the truth, I can only speculate that

Daddy was concerned with my mortality and whether or not he would allow me to keep it.

I'm certain that had to be the angriest I have ever encountered Daddy to be. All I could hope and pray for was that he would cool down on his way to Cartersville to pick me up. My buddy shared the same thoughts as mine as he awaited his father's arrival. When Daddy showed up at the train station, he met me with a warm embrace and exclamations of how glad he was that I was okay. When we got home, the only warmness I felt was on my hind end as Daddy applied his 32-inch belt across it. By now, that belt and I had gotten to know each other fairly well. I never hopped on a train again after that day.

****

On one particular steamy hot summer day, I invited a friend, Barry Owen, "over to play", as we used to call it. Looking for something to do, Barry and I cooked up a not-so-dangerous but ultra-devious and desperate plot to obtain the funding we needed to purchase a few packs of baseball cards. Since I was a knee high to a grasshopper, I had been collecting baseball cards. I didn't quite understand that these cardboard collectibles of staged photos and statistics of the major leaguers would one day have value, particularly those of the game's greats or those who were rookies and who would one day go on to stardom.

The only significance to me, that the cards held, was that they sounded cool when I would attach one of them to my bicycle wheel spokes with a clothespin and the rattling sound it would make when I would ride my bike all over Rockmart. The hard stick of powdery bubble gum didn't taste half-bad either, although its flavor only lasted about fifteen seconds. Barry and I needed money, and we devised a plan that would surely capture the hearts of my neighbors on Ivy Street and that, ultimately, would provide Barry and me with the resources needed to purchase several packs of our favorite brand of baseball cards, Topps.

Barry and I scrounged up one of Momma's plain white envelopes that she used monthly to pay bills with. Putting forth my best effort in writing professionally and legibly, and using the spelling skills I had honed in elementary school, (I actually went on to place highly in every school spelling bee I ever participated in) I penned the words "Kansur Society" on the front of the envelope. Barry and I then set out on our journey of knocking on each and every door on Ivy Street, batting our baby blues and playing the con game on all of my naïve and unsuspecting neighbors; well, at least that's what our little pea brains thought.

William and Mary Lumpkin lived two doors down from us on Ivy Street. William worked for one of the two large railroad companies whose trains ran through Rockmart, and was one of the funniest men I've ever known, always cracking jokes and making funny faces. Mary was a nurse and caregiver but, to me, she was much more than that.

Mary thought the sun rose and set in my eyes, and she always showed that to me. When she would see me, she would hug and kiss on me with no inhibitions. Mary sweated a lot, particularly in her head. I can remember her perspiration oozing down my round, chubby face, blending in to my own sweat, as she would squeeze me up against her rosy cheeks.

I cherished the love that Mary always gave me, so I knew that Mary adored me enough to give Barry and me at least a dollar for the "Kansur Society". Sure enough, after a few hugs and kisses, Mary doled out four quarters, a whole dollar total. What we didn't count on, as we departed the shaded screened porch of the Lumpkin's Southern-style home, was that Mary would phone Momma to tell her that she had given the money to Barry and me. Mary was on to our high jinks but she didn't want to tell me no; she would let Momma handle that.

Only two doors down from our home, I heard Momma's stern cry of, "BRAD HULSEY! YOU GET YOURSELF HOME RIGHT NOW!". I wasn't sure, but I suspected that the jig was up. Sure enough – it was! After Barry's parents picked him up from the house, only minutes after Momma had cried out for me, I had the solemn honor of going out into the yard and "picking a switch," with which Momma cleaned the leaves off of and began blistering my rear end and legs.

After weeping uncontrollably from Momma's fit of rage and wrath, and in between deep and gasping breaths, I apologized for the error of my ways. Once Momma "cooled down", she told me that Mary had called her and told her about Barry's and my escapades. She then directed me to go back to my door-to-door jaunt and to return all of my ill-gotten finances. I returned all of the money, along with an apology to my neighbors who had given. I imagine most, if not all of them knew that they were part of our Ponzi scheme. God love them!

That was a difficult learning experience, one in which I received grace beyond measure from the good folks in our neighborhood, especially Mary. When I got to her front door steps Mary, as always, greeted me with a loving, sweaty hug and sweet kiss on the top of my head as she held me.

In a moment of shame and contrition, I wept in Mary's loving arms. She told me that all would be fine, and that all was forgiven with her. I handed Mary the four quarters I thought I had swindled her out of, and she proceeded to stuff two of them back into my shorts pocket. "Now go and buy you some baseball cards, Sweetheart," Mary adoringly told me. I had made it through the ordeal with a blistered buttock and legs, and an appreciation for the love of our neighbors. Little did I know the impact "kansur" would have on the Hulsey family one day.

****

I had the fortune of growing up in a neighborhood where neighbor loved and cared about neighbor. Back then, there was no such thing as an automatic garage door; in fact, most everyone didn't have a garage and, if they did (just like my family) it was detached from the house. Newer homes had carports attached to their structure. Our neighborhood was built primarily back in the 1920s and 1930s, with a few homes scattered about that were constructed later on, but no homes had a carport.

When Momma and Daddy would come home from work, they couldn't hide as we do these days by exiting their car inside a closed garage door. You had to walk up to your house, rain or shine, from your car and, usually, you stopped to say hello to a neighbor, young or old, who was outside of their house.

The kids in the neighborhood, including Phil and me, would always say hello to our adult neighbors and, for that matter, anyone who passed down the scenic sidewalks and streets that encompassed our little neck of the woods in Rockmart; well, except for one person. There was a particular man who occasionally would walk down our street whom we didn't know anything about, only that he was dirty, wore tattered clothing and, for us, was a scary sight.

This unkempt fellow would stroll rapidly with his head down, taking long strides even though he was short in stature. When you spoke to him, he never acknowledged you, and we would shout at him to get him to notice us. He never would. In his right hip pocket, he carried an empty jar of Orange Tang drink mix with a rusty lid, filled with loose coins.

Phil and I sometimes wondered if this was the infamous "Goat Man," a traveling preacher who became a folk and religious figure in Georgia for more than four decades, and who influenced the works of the writer Flannery O'Connor. We only thought this because this reserved, curious and unshaven man looked like the photos we had seen of Goat Man.

Years later, I would learn that this poor soul had lost all of his family over time, and that he had lived out the remainder of his days, sad and lonely. No one could recall his name, and there was no family or recorded information.

Clifford Fambro, who was our next-door neighbor for several years, lived to be 101-years old. Mr. Fambro was an interesting soul, who loved sipping his wine from time to time (but never overconsuming), talking to anyone and everyone that crossed his path, and playing golf. His wife, Mattie Lane Fambro, was a true Southern Belle who loved and doted on Phil and me. When their granddaughter, Nancy McRae, would come over for a visit, "Ms. Mattie," as we affectionately called Mrs. Fambro, would make the best Rice Krispies marshmallow treats ever for us to enjoy as we played "house".

Phil always got to play the role of husband to Nancy by threatening to beat me up. I, in turn, would have to settle for the role of their son. We would roam up and down the sidewalks and back alleys of Ivy Street, acting as if we were grownups, and all the while Phil would tell me what to do, like a good father did.

We designated our "house" as an open spot in the long row of thick privet hedge just behind the Fambro dwelling. There, we would prepare our meals of leaves, rocks and sticks. We would pretend to thoroughly enjoy the feast set before us; that is, until Ms. Mattie would call us in for the tasty, sweet marshmallow treats.

Being a retired educator, Ms. Mattie had quite the collection of children's books. She would read those books to us as we polished off the remainder of the treats. She was the first person I ever knew who, in my small-sized brain's method of thinking, had to wait an entire year for her birthday. She was born on December 31, 1895, so I surmised that since she was born on New Year's Eve, she had to wait longer than anyone else to gain another year of age. Ms. Mattie passed away in 1972, a great loss to so many, including me, who loved her dearly.

Both Mr. and Mrs. Fambro had experienced and seen so much transpire over their years of growing up and living in Rockmart. I've often wondered if they knew my Hulsey grandfathers, and why they didn't speak of them. They must have known them. Did they ever socialize with them? Did they know any details about their lives? Whether they did or didn't, they never spoke of them or any other Hulseys, for that matter. All they did was be loving and caring neighbors.

****

During my childhood years, Rockmart was a diverse city, with a near-even mixture of whites and blacks inhabiting the community. Growing up in a small southern town in the 1960's and 1970's provided a skewed view of what life should have been like in a free American society.

60 CENTS

As a young boy, our family always had a maid that would come to our home often during the weekdays. One in particular, Mattie Nettles, was near and dear to my heart. Either Momma or Daddy would have to travel the 1.5-mile trek to Mattie's humble frame house to pick her up and take her back home. I don't even know if Mattie was married, but I do know that she never owned a vehicle.

The area Mattie and most all of the black citizens of Rockmart inhabited was located literally "across the tracks," a phrase to describe where people of color and/or poor people lived in a segregated society. There were other abhorrent names given to that area of town, as well. As a boy, I constantly wondered why Mattie and the other black folks didn't reside within our neighborhoods, why they didn't attend the same churches as us, and why my parents and their friends didn't socialize with them.

Mattie's home stood right next to the railroad tracks that led to Birmingham. Segregation was a part of our culture in Rockmart in those days, something that I saw but couldn't comprehend. All I knew is that I loved "my Mattie," and I couldn't wait for her to come to our residence.

At our house, Mattie would vacuum, sweep and mop floors, wash and dry clothes, prepare meals for Phil and me while Momma and Daddy were at work, and perform other domestic-type chores. I know that Momma paid Mattie a wage, but I'm sure it was some minuscule amount.

When Mattie would complete the required tasks she had been assigned, she would always take time to dote over me.

I was affectionately called "the baby" by Mattie, an appellation that I found love, comfort – and, opportunity in. In her eyes, I could do no wrong.

When misconduct would prevail between Phil and me, all I had to do was turn on the tears, and Mattie would come to my defense, scolding poor ole Phil for something he perhaps had little or nothing to do with. Eventually, Mattie would leave us and begin working for the Atha family in Rockmart. They would offer her more hours and, therefore, higher pay. We would have other maids, but none more special to me than "my Mattie".

There was other evidence of a racial divide in Rockmart during those times. Our schools had become integrated only a few years prior to my elementary school days, primarily due to President Lyndon B. Johnson's sweeping Civil Rights Act of 1964. Before then, black children in Rockmart would attend Elm Street School, while the white students would attend several segregated schools within the community. Elm Street School would eventually become integrated as Rockmart Junior High, where I attended grades 6 through 8.

Many of the black students excelled in academia, and while many of the locals didn't like that our schools had become integrated, those sentiments would take a back seat to the exuberating thrills they would often experience on a cool, crisp autumn Friday evening. That would be when one of the high school's black football players was displaying his exceptional athletic prowess on the gridiron at Rockmart High's Hilburn Field.

As one of the black running backs would dash down the field for a touchdown, many of the townsfolk would be shouting their praises toward them. When that same running back would fumble the ball or get tackled for a loss, racial slurs would be slung at them by some of those same people, a stark contrast to what they had been exclaiming only minutes before.

Rockmart had two public swimming pools during my childhood days. The Rockmart Pool, located in downtown Rockmart, was for the enjoyment of whites only. The blacks had their own separate pool located adjacent to the Elm Street/Rockmart Junior High School.

The Rockmart Pool was walking distance from our home on Ivy Street. Phil, our friends and I would journey down to the blue-painted cement pool on many a summer's day for a dip. It was a vast structure, one that featured a proportional shallow end and deep end. For the smaller children and toddlers, there was also the "baby pool" for them to enjoy. There, we would watch many of the teen boys and girls hurl themselves into the deep water from either the low or high diving board.

When someone would thrust themselves from the high dive, the board would make a loud, distinctive sound that we could hear from our front porch on Ivy Street, about a half-mile away. Conversely, the black-only pool was very small, similar to one that would be constructed in a private backyard. There were no diving boards, probably a blessing in disguise, since there would tend to be a multitude of children and teens occupying the pool that appeared to make it impossible to actually swim in, much less dive into.

While I knew that there was a racial and cultural divide between blacks and whites within our community, that didn't stop me and my white buddies from becoming close friends with many of the black children that we attended school with. We affectionately called each other "brother" or "sister".

Contrary to the sentiments that many southern white folks espoused, it didn't appear to bother Momma and Daddy when I would invite one of my black brethren home with me to play. During the summer break from school, when my buddies, black and white, would hook up for a day of fun and fellowship, we would "whip" the socially accepted system of segregating swimming facilities.

On the southern end of downtown Rockmart there is a small dam on the Euharlee Creek. The intake pipes for the Rockmart water system were located there along with a pump house that siphoned the raw water from the Euharlee and pumped it northerly to the Water Treatment Plant. At the base of the dam was a deep swimming hole where my friends, both black and white, and I could enjoy a frolicking plunge into our faithful water source.

There, we could simply be kids, without any of the trappings and barriers associated with the racial biases and edicts that dictated interaction between blacks and whites. Those experiences made for a lifetime of solid friendships. We didn't see each other as black and white – we looked at each other as devoted brothers and sisters – all living in that same small town.

CHAPTER TWO: DADDY

There was always the public side of Daddy, and then there was the private side of him, one that I didn't truly understand for decades. I believe the same held true for my Granddaddy Hulsey. Fred Avery Hulsey, Jr., my father, was born in Aragon, Georgia, three miles outside of Rockmart, on August 15, 1924, the oldest child of Fred Avery Hulsey, Sr. and Verdie Mae Locklear Hulsey, my Granddaddy and Grandmother Hulsey. Granddaddy and Maw Maw Vert, as we called our dear grandmother, were married on December 1, 1923.

The best I can figure, Maw Maw Vert was already pregnant with Daddy when she and Granddaddy tied the knot of matrimony. Oh well, at least they got married and had the baby. Come to think of it, I wouldn't be here had they not.

Granddaddy Hulsey was at the ripe young age of twenty-three when Daddy came into the world. Maw Maw Vert was even riper, having turned the tender young age of seventeen one week prior to Daddy's birth. Granddaddy and Maw Maw would conceive three more children. Daddy was the oldest, and his sister, Hope, born on June 26, 1929, would be the youngest.

Hope would eventually marry a local World War II hero, J.R. Woods, and together they would live in Rockmart, raising four children: Diana, Jeff, Don and Julia. They would be the only first cousins Phil and I would have on the Hulsey side of our family. Each one of them has a wonderful sense of humor and wit about them.

We've never been a very close-knit family, but they are my flesh and blood, and I love them deeply. Since their last name is Woods, they don't have to carry on the Hulsey name like Daddy, Phil and I do. In some ways, that may be a blessing for them.

Daddy loved to tell stories of his childhood and teenage memories of Boy Scouts, swimming in the Euharlee Creek, frog gigging in the local streams and ponds, roller skating through the town until his skates were completely worn down, and sports – oh how Daddy loved sports. Daddy excelled at the highest level athletically, particularly in football. He was small in stature, just like Granddaddy Hulsey was purported to be.

Daddy never got above 170 pounds soaking wet with a sack of potatoes in each of his hands, but what he lacked in size he made up with muscle, quickness, and an endless measure of courage and determination. More than one person has shared memories of Daddy completely leaping over fourteen men squatting side-by-side on their knees, with their heads down, all the while hoping and praying that he wouldn't land on top of them.

I have heard stories of Daddy having run through players twice his size while playing quarterback for the Fighting Yellow Jackets of Rockmart High School. Daddy used to tell us the story of how he ran a punt return back eighty yards for the game-winning touchdown against Rockmart High's archrival, the Cedartown Bulldogs. Daddy said grown men were carrying him on their shoulders and that others were flipping five and ten dollar bills at him. No way could you get away with that these days.

I'm sure Granddaddy Hulsey would have been beaming with pride after watching his son become the hometown hero. But he wasn't there to bask in all of Daddy's glory with him. He had left this earth way too soon, at the age of thirty-one, and he never got to see Daddy's athletic prowess or, later, his achievements in so many other areas of his life. Granddaddy Hulsey never got to see, or hold, or play with, any of his six grandchildren. As a child, I always wondered what had happened to him. It took me longer than I ever expected to discover the truth.

Rose Hill is the largest cemetery in Rockmart. Many of Rockmart's most famous (well, at least to home folks) and historical citizens are buried there. Among the thousands interred there is Colonel Seaborn Jones, who is credited with being the founder of Rockmart, in 1872. Colonel Jones was a well-respected and wealthy landowner who donated much of the land that encompasses the city limits. On the west side of the cemetery, the Hulsey family burial plot can be found.

Along with Maw Maw Vert, Daddy took Phil and me there when we were little boys. The cool winds were whisking over the hill as we gazed upon the headstones of our deceased ancestors. The howling sound of the winds made for an eerie feeling as I drew closer to Maw Maw's comforting hug, and her sweet smell. She always smelled like a flower garden.

One of the headstones read, "William R. Hulsey, February 9, 1926-November 27, 1926". I inquired of Maw Maw Vert who this person was. Daddy swiftly came to her rescue (the family was always "protecting" Maw Maw, even though she was much stronger than they gave her credit for). Daddy grievously shared the sad story that little William was his younger brother. Evidently, William was at the stage of early childhood development where he was just learning to pull himself up. On November 27, 1926, William held tightly to the family stove as he attempted to pull himself up vertically. On top of the stove was a boiling pot of water, and before anyone could react to save him, little William tipped the water over onto his wee, tiny body, scalding himself to death at only nearly ten-months of age.

There was another gravestone that simply read, "Marion Hulsey – 1927". Daddy sorrowfully bowed his head and pronounced that this was his oldest sister; one that he never knew…. she was stillborn. Maw Maw just stood there with tears streaming down her face as Daddy told us about those heart-wrenching occurrences. Surely Granddaddy Hulsey was devastated by what had happened to these two precious offspring of his. Or was he? Surely to goodness he was. I know he had to love Daddy and Aunt Hope – his own living children. Surely he was unselfish and doted on them. Or did he?

In the rear of the Hulsey family plot stands a headstone

that has engraved upon it, "Fred A. Hulsey, 1901-1932". As an impressionable little tyke, this was an eye-opening experience, gazing upon my father's name in a cemetery at the head of a grave. I began to wonder why Daddy's name would be there, since he was standing right in front of me. He surely wasn't dead, was he? I could see him...I could hear him...I could feel him. Daddy cracked a smile and let me know that this was the grave of his father, Fred A. Hulsey, Sr., and that he was named for his father; thus, Fred A. Hulsey, Jr.

Being a curious little lad, I asked Daddy why his daddy had died at such an early age. Without hesitation, and with Maw Maw Vert listening intently along with Phil and me, Daddy exclaimed that Fred Sr. – Granddaddy Hulsey – had died at such an early age of a heart attack. For me, at that stage of my life, that was a good enough explanation.

I would believe for over two decades that Granddaddy Hulsey had died from a heart attack, and at the ripe old age of thirty-one. It made sense to me. Most men died from a heart attack or some illness or accident. What did I know? I was just a kid, who took every word from his father's mouth as the gospel truth. He was my Daddy, and he was consistently on the up-and-up. I had no reason to question him. His word was final, and I believed anything and everything he told me. After all, that is what good sons are supposed to do – listen to and believe in their fathers...right?

There at the family plot, Maw Maw Vert revealed to me that Granddaddy Hulsey was so excited to have a son when

Daddy was born, and that he wanted him named for him. When William Robert was born, he was partly named for Great-Granddaddy Hulsey, whose name was William Avery Hulsey.

Most all of the Hulsey men, throughout the lineage, are partially named for a family relative, with the exception of one – yours truly. Just one more reason for me to feel omitted and betrayed by my own flesh and blood. I was given my own unique name, but I've often wondered why I couldn't have been named for my father, Fred Avery Hulsey III? I mean, Brad Alan Hulsey is okay. Phil – Phillip Edward Hulsey – was named for a family friend, Phillip Kinney, and two of our maternal uncles, Lum Edward Holland and William Edward Hardy.

So why couldn't I bear the full name of my father, his father, or even my Great-Granddaddy Hulsey, and be like all of the other Hulsey men? I would determine years later that having the Hulsey name was more than enough and that, perhaps, it was in my best interest to not become my father's, my grandfather's or my great-grandfather's name-sake.

Daddy and I would not discuss Granddaddy or Great-Granddaddy Hulsey for several years after that day. I thought I had gotten all the information I needed at the time. As time passed, and as circumstances changed, I would learn later that I had only gotten a tidbit of what I would one day discover.

As a pre-teen, and being the curious sort that just had to

know every little detail about certain things, my interest peaked once again about my Hulsey relatives. What I hadn't realized until that time was that I had never known any Hulsey blood relatives aside from Daddy and Phil. People would ask if I was kin to this Hulsey or that Hulsey, and I had no clue whatsoever if I was or not. I wanted to know, and I felt that I had a right to know.

I interrogated Daddy about our Hulsey relatives, and he said that we were the only Hulseys left of our blood lineage and that the rest had died. I believed what Daddy was saying. After all, he was my father, and I had always trusted him and his word.

I once quizzed Daddy as to what kind of man Granddaddy Hulsey was. I wanted to know what he looked like, how he talked, what he did for a living, what his favorite ice cream flavor was, what he wore, what his voice sounded like, what his favorite sport was, and so on. I wanted to know everything. The things that Daddy told me about his father, my Granddaddy Hulsey, created more questions in my puzzled mind than it provided answers.

Daddy stated that Granddaddy was considered a nice man by many, even going as far as to say that he was considered a good man by most people. He said he was a sharp dresser, and that he liked having his clothes mono-grammed – FH, for Fred Hulsey.

Daddy went on to share that Granddaddy worked in a local grocery store up on the Goodyear corner (Goodyear Avenue and Piedmont Avenue) in Rockmart, and that he was considered one of the best meat butchers around. He also worked at Great-Granddaddy's farm, just outside of Rockmart in a small community known as Van Wert.

Daddy described Granddaddy as "a man about town," who would always speak to the town folks and give them a hearty wave and firm handshake when approaching them. Daddy went on to say that it was when Granddaddy and Great-Granddaddy Hulsey would do things in tandem that Granddaddy would be considered at his worst. He didn't expound beyond that statement, simply shrugging it off as the way things were.

This really got my inquisitive brain going. I wondered what Granddaddy and Great-Granddaddy had gotten into over the years. But it seemed obvious to me that it couldn't have been anything serious. Surely if that were the case, I would have heard about it from Daddy, Momma, Maw Maw Vert or any of the townspeople. Wouldn't they have told me?

I surmised that Granddaddy and Great-Granddaddy Hulsey were mischievous, just like I was. No harm – no foul. I thought to myself, "Getting into a little mischief wasn't the end of the world, as long as it wasn't breaking the law, even if the law may have been stretched to its' furthest limit". Although I never met either one of them, besides the surname of Hulsey, I had discovered a bond with my Hulsey grandfathers. I was like them – or was I?

After continuously quizzing Daddy about what Great-Granddaddy Hulsey was like, Daddy opened up about him. What happened then was shocking and surprising and, yes, very confusing to me. On top of all that, it scared me and made me fear Daddy like I had never before.

Daddy had a strange look in his eyes, and he was visibly shaking. I noticed a tear running down his beet-red face as he began flailing his arms high into the room, almost as if he wanted to hit something or, even worse...me. In an angry and tempestuous voice Daddy looked at me and exclaimed, "Son, don't you ever ask me about him again! He was the biggest son-of-a-bitch who ever lived, so much so that they buried him in an unmarked grave!"

Okay then – I figured out very quickly that I'd better not go there again! I had pushed the wrong buttons. Daddy would never apologize for nor mention that outburst – ever. At that time, I had no understanding of what had happened. I could not understand why Daddy felt that way about Great-Granddaddy Hulsey. I would deposit it away into my own memory bank, but I couldn't hide it from my soul. His words would reverberate through my innermost being, and they still do. I knew, one day, that I would have to make a withdrawal from my memory bank and find out what this was all about.

I wanted to know if I possessed any of the characteristics or personality of Granddaddy Hulsey or, God forbid, Great-Granddaddy Hulsey. Far be it that I would be known as a son-of-a-bitch and, worse still, be buried in an unmarked grave. How shameful is all of that? Why would anyone say that? Why would my own father say that, especially?

That particular episode created a plethora of wonderment

in my mind. I wanted to know; no, I needed to know what this hullabaloo surrounding my Great-Granddaddy was all about. Besides my fascination, it brought about a flashback to something that had occurred in a neighbor's yard near Ivy Street several years prior.

Fred Braswell was the Mayor of Rockmart for many years. Aside from being Mayor, he had served on the Rockmart City Council, the Polk County School Board, the Board of Directors of the Rockmart Bank, and on various other civic and church-related boards. He owned and operated Braswell's Food Market for fifty-five years. Mayor Braswell was a fine leader and an even finer human being. He and his wife, the former Martha Jane Abernathy, lived on Central Street in a beautiful home up on a hill that was rock-throwing distance from our backyard.

As a child, I just knew that the Braswell home was, in reality, the Mayor's Mansion. It was the home that the citizens of Rockmart had provided for their leader – no different from the Governor's Mansion in Atlanta or the White House in Washington, D.C. However, I never could figure out why Mayor Braswell always drove himself, and where his bodyguards were stationed. I just assumed they were doing a good job of hiding, ready to shoot any unknown intruder or would-be assassin that would want to get the Honorable Mayor.

The Braswell's front yard was heavily-wooded, and it had several large boulders that were securely affixed into the ground. This was a prime area to play hide-and-seek. We would play Army, as we called it, as well. We acted as if we were great warriors of the United States, fighting the mighty battles to protect our sacred country. I don't know why we didn't call it "playing Marines", since Daddy was a veteran of the United States Marine Corps.

One afternoon, Phil and I meandered our way up through our backyard and up the hill of the Braswell's. As Phil covered his eyes and began counting—one Mississippi...two Mississippi...three Mississippi—and as I went to hide behind one of the massive trees on the Braswell property, we heard the loud, shrill voice of a crotchety, elderly female neighbor of ours, Ms. Elizabeth Carter.

Shouting out at the top of her lungs, Ms. Carter exclaimed, "Get out of that yard right now, and don't you ever come back! You boys are nothing but old Hulseys!" Phil and I scampered down the hill as fast as we could, our hearts pounding and thinking all the while, "feet don't fail me now!"

We darted through the screened door located on the back porch of our house, and slammed it and the main door behind us as fast as we could. We hoped that if the old curmudgeon was still running after us we could keep her out. Phil and I could barely catch our breath nor hold back the tears of fear and hurt that grumpy old Ms. Carter had stirred with her actions and words.

Daddy came into the kitchen where we were, and through our gasping for air, we apprised him of what had just taken place. He put his arms around us as if to calm and comfort my brother and me and then, turning us around and looking straight into our eyes, he coolly said, "Oh, boys, don't worry about that, and don't concern yourselves with what that old sourpuss said to you. She's just a mean old lady, and you needn't worry about her."

I learned years later that Daddy went straight to Fred Braswell and told him about the episode, and that Mayor Braswell was very apologetic and embarrassed over what had taken place. As far as he was concerned, Phil and I were always welcome to play in their yard. Nevertheless, to be called "old Hulseys" stuck to me. I would and could never forget it. What did Ms. Carter mean? What was wrong with being a Hulsey? Why would she have even said such a thing? And, why did Daddy say such horrible things about Great-Granddaddy Hulsey?

It was a mystery—a secret that I couldn't wrap my arms around and embrace. I wanted to know, but I was becoming too afraid to find out. Would I ever know? I would have to walk away from my curiosity – well, at least for a while. It would be longer than I anticipated.

****

When Daddy wasn't at work at Goodyear, where he served as paymaster for the salaried employees and had responsibility for accounting of all payroll records, he was always busy doing other things. It was rare for him to not be doing something with his "spare" time, including his inability to "spare" much time for me, particularly during my pre-teen and teenage years.

Daddy was heavily involved with the Rockmart Little

League baseball program. Even before Phil and I were born and eventually playing in the league ourselves, Daddy had served as a coach for several teams, and in various leadership roles on the League's Board of Directors. He spent a good amount of his "spare" time at the Little League field, volunteering an overabundance of his time and effort into seeing that all went off without a hitch as we young men played baseball.

To the extent that Daddy, through his leadership and efforts was helping make for a better Little League experience for me, Phil and all of the other boys (there were one or two girls playing, as well), it made me grateful for his willingness to serve. But given the fact that he was always so busy, not able to spend time with me, not attending most of my ballgames, and not allowing a listening ear as I sought to recap my accomplishments on the baseball diamond for any particular given day, or week, or season – I felt like Daddy had abandoned me, and that I, as his son, didn't mean as much to him.

I love baseball. I love the strategy that is part of the game, and I love the competitiveness. The game would eventually help me hone skills that have carried on throughout my life, particularly: the strategizing; the coaching; the "having a good eye" on any person or project I may encounter; the ability to handle failure (after all, getting a hit three out of ten attempts over a career normally puts you into the Hall of Fame, unless you're Pete Rose or a steroid-era player); and, learning how to be humble in victory and to handle defeat productively. All of these lessons and many others I have learned through the game of baseball have helped to build my character and enhanced my ability to excel as an adult.

Unlike Daddy, I wasn't much of a football player. In fact, I never played high school football, only midget football, when I was much younger. But baseball – well, I could commit my heart, soul and mind to that game. I never was a superstar, but I played well enough to make the All-Star team on three occasions, and I played my senior year in high school for the Rockmart Yellow Jackets. While I didn't play much that year, I did see some action during the games.

Coach Ken Jolly was our head coach that year. He had been an accomplished pitcher, having pitched for a short stint in the Major League for the Philadelphia Phillies. Coach Jolly was firm with our team and expected excellence both on and off the ballfield. He cared if we were doing our schoolwork, if we were involved in other school-sponsored activities, and he cared about our lives. Coach Jolly told me that he had picked me for the team not for my abilities, but for my mind. He saw in me a baseball thinker, a strategist, a coach, and hustler, and someone with the drive to excel and win. I appreciated his believing in me enough to make me a member of the team.

I could only wish that Daddy would have thought of me in the same manner Coach Jolly did. How could I show that to him? I wanted so desperately for Daddy to believe all of those things about me, and more. I just wanted him to notice me...period.

60 CENTS

Daddy never came to a single one of my high school baseball games. He was always busy doing something else, usually at the Little League field. After twenty years of service in various positions, Daddy had risen to the top of leadership as President of the Rockmart Little League. He was so busy giving his time, talents and abilities to the Little League that he forgot to be busy paying attention to his son.

All at once, I was both proud and resentful of Daddy. I was proud that he was playing a vital role in the lives of so many young boys and girls; and, I was resentful of the fact that, of all of those young kids, he seemed to have forgotten about his own flesh and blood. Every young man desires the attention and approval of his father. Daddy had never gotten that from Granddaddy Hulsey but, hey, that wasn't my fault. I would somehow need to get it from Daddy.

****

The lunches that we were being served at Rockmart High School were, let's say, downright atrocious. I wouldn't have fed much of the food to my own dog. Most of what the lunchroom staff was preparing was government-issued. It wasn't the staff's fault that the quality of what they were feeding us was not up to par. They had very little say-so as to what food would be sent their way to prepare for us students. All of that "came down from on high" from the powers that be at the Polk County School District, the Georgia Department of Agriculture, the U.S. Department of Agriculture and the Food and Drug Administration.

BRAD HULSEY

I was in my senior year (12th grade) at Rockmart High that year (1978-1979), and had been elected by my classmates, the Class of 1979, as Senior Class President (I had been elected Junior Class President the year before and Sophomore Class Vice-President two years before, as well). Daddy never seemed overly impressed with my positions in high school.

I distinctly recall being served turkey one day in the lunch line, along with green beans, mashed potatoes (usually a daily staple) and some of Mattie Lee Alexander's homemade rolls that were to die for! I ate my rolls, and when I went back into the line with my cunning smile and batting my baby blue eyes, Mattie Lee sneaked me a couple of extra rolls, handing them over with a wink and a nod.

It was the turkey that I just couldn't touch, nor could anyone else, for that matter. No doubt, the turkey had been processed, probably ground up with all of the turkey parts, everything except the breast, and formed into a sliced piece of undetectable meat. The texture was like rubber, and you could literally see through the meat, as if it was clear in color.

This was nothing new about the meals that we were being served. It had been going on for quite some time. As the leader of the Senior Class of Rockmart High, and as a young teenage guy who was still in need of getting his Daddy's attention, I devised a plan for, hopefully, getting the quality of the lunches up to par at Rockmart High and, ultimately, getting Daddy to notice me, once and for all.

60 CENTS

One day during lunch break, soon after the turkey fiasco, I gathered a cross section of the student body in the courtyard at the high school. I had constructed makeshift protest signs that exclaimed something ultra-profound upon them: "WE WANT BETTER LUNCHES!" Man, I went all out on that one!

I gathered up my posse and led them from the front in a march for better lunches to the Principal's Office. Brandishing the signs, we entered into and marched through the main building of the school (where some classes were in progress) chanting, "WE WANT BETTER LUNCHES! WE WANT BETTER LUNCHES!"

We were met outside the school office door where the Principal's Office was located by none other than "the man" himself, our esteemed principal, Mr. Bill Keller. Mr. Keller had been a former head football coach at Rockmart High School, and he had "that look" that only a rough and rugged football coach has – big forearms, a stern upper lip, broad shoulders, and a stare that would knock you down!

Mr. Keller's wife, Ann, was one of my favorite teachers ever. She taught me in the fifth grade at Euharlee School, and we have since felt like kindred spirits since we both share the same birthdate, October 28th. I don't believe I gave Mrs. Keller as much trouble as I did her husband.

Having taken the role of leader and having not backed down from my principles to the Principal, so to speak, I was the first (and only) to meet eyeball-to-eyeball with Mr. Keller. As he gave me "the stare" through his soda bottle glasses, I knew it was all about to go down – way down on my account.

Mr. Keller quizzed me, "What are you doing?" I responded, "Just trying to get some improvements to the lunches here, Mr. Keller. That's all." Mr. Keller retorted, "Mr. Hulsey, this isn't the way to get anything accomplished...leading a march! Now, you and your legion get on back to your classrooms, and quit disrupting my school!"

I stood and gazed into Mr. Keller's eyes, only for a brief moment. Through the anger I saw in those eyes, I caught a subtle smile from one side of his mouth. I told my posse that it was time to leave, and we quickly departed.

About fifteen minutes after the march and after having returned to the classroom to attempt to continue my education for the day, Mr. Keller's voice rang out over the school intercom... "YOUR ATTENTION PLEASE, YOUR ATTENTION! BRAD HULSEY...BRAD HULSEY, PLEASE REPORT TO THE PRINCIPAL'S OFFICE AT ONCE!" Uh-oh, here it goes! He's had time to digest the situation, and Mr. Keller has determined that I needed to be punished. I knew this would get Daddy's attention, but not in the way I had imagined or wanted it.

As I left the classroom, I started stuffing the back pockets of my jeans with notebook paper, just in case I was going to receive the wrath of Mr. Keller's world-famous paddle. My classmates oohed and aahed and laughed at my pending doom as I walked out of the classroom, my pockets bulging with my paper-laden, shock-absorbing padding.

60 CENTS

Mr. Keller greeted me at the front door of the school office, and invited me in to his private office. This was not a place you would ever endeavor to be in.

Mr. Keller asked me to take a seat but, before I did, to take the folded stash of notebook paper out of my back pockets. There would be no paddling today. I nervously sat down across from Mr. Keller. He was sitting upright at his desk filled with papers and an office decorated with photo memories and trophies from championships gone by. I sensed from his disposition that he wasn't angry.

Mr. Keller asked me why I had led the march, and what the deal was about the lunches. I quickly brought up the turkey, and he stopped me in mid-sentence. Mr. Keller exclaimed, "Brad, I remember that turkey. It was awful! I couldn't eat it and, in fact, the only thing I ate that day was Mattie Lee's rolls!" The principal and I had made a connection.

Mr. Keller and I bantered back and forth about the lunches, about the lunchroom appearance and ambiance, and just about everything else imaginable related to the school. At the end of the conversation, Mr. Keller advised me that he would support me forming a Nutrition Council, composed of students of my choosing from each high school class (freshman, sophomore, junior and senior) whose objective would be to work with lunchroom staff, a couple of teachers of his choosing, and a representative from the Polk County School District toward making improvements in all aspects of the lunch program and the lunchroom "experience."

We were to report our findings and recommendations to Mr. Keller at the appropriate time. Our principal had listened to us, and he gave us an opportunity to show what we were made of. Who could ask for more than that?

I got busy forming the Nutrition Council. Momma had found out "through the grapevine," like all Rockmart mothers somehow did, and confronted me about my leading the march and the subsequent support of Mr. Keller. I asked her if Daddy knew about it, and she said that, to the best of her knowledge, he didn't. I thought, "Good! Let's leave it that way for now!"

After forming the Nutrition Council, and our having met with all of the persons Mr. Keller had outlined in his proposal, the Council had a plan in place that was unanimously acceptable to the Council, the teachers, and the Polk County School District representative. All we needed now was Mr. Keller's blessings.

The Nutrition Council presented the following recommendations for improvements to the lunchroom ambiance, and to the quality of the lunches: all walls in the lunchroom were to be painted a brighter color; the floors in the lunchroom were to be cleaned and waxed more frequently; the lighting in the lunchroom was to be upgraded to provide more brightness; a jukebox, filled with records of music with taste but that teenagers enjoy would be placed in the lunchroom, to be paid for with revenues derived by students paying for the songs; a salad bar would now be offered as an alternative meal for students, having only been offered to faculty and staff in the past; chocolate milk would be offered along with the standard whole milk; and, finally, students would be able to purchase ice cream products during lunchroom hours.

After hearing our recommendations, Mr. Keller didn't hesitate in saying yes to all of them. From a staged march, to being sent back to our classrooms, to a one-on-one conversation between Mr. Keller and me, to the formation of the Nutrition Council and the subsequent meetings, recommendations and report, we had made a difference, and I had led the process. I was proud of myself, and I hoped that Daddy would be.

The local newspaper, *The Rockmart Journal*, wrote a feature story on the formation and work of the Nutrition Council and the resulting outcome. They ran photos of all of us with the feature story.

As far as I knew, until the story ran, Daddy had no clue what had taken place. I was correct. He hadn't known, and when he read the article and saw the photos, he was unimpressed with what I had done. I wondered to myself – what does it take to impress Daddy? Why can't I make my mark with him? Was it that nothing could move my father in a news article quite like stories from years gone by could? Did it all stem from his not having his own father to praise him when he had accomplished something in his life? If only I knew.

BRAD HULSEY

Fred Avery Hulsey, Jr. (Daddy)

Daddy, Maw Maw Vert and Aunt Hope

60 CENTS

Fred Avery Hulsey, Sr.
(Granddaddy)

William Avery Hulsey
(Great-Granddaddy)

CHAPTER THREE:
'STUDY' ABROAD

I did make an impression with Daddy – and Momma, with another high school antic just before my senior year. It was another one of my countless capers and, needless to say, they didn't see my continued mischief as impressive. The fact that I got caught this time was difficult to fathom and still is to this day. Throughout my life, I have had the tendency of being at the wrong place at the wrong time. I was told by Daddy that this was analogous to having the Hulsey name.

I was doomed for being captured in misconduct, just like the "Kansur" Society escapade from my younger days. At Rockmart High School, I excelled in foreign languages, namely Spanish and French. I had much higher grades in the three Spanish classes and three French classes I participated in than I did in English classes over my four-year stint at Rockmart High.

Mary Ann Bennett was the teacher of foreign languages, and I simply adored her. Mrs. Bennett had taught for many years prior to my arriving at Rockmart High School in 1975. She was renowned for her crooked, arthritic fingers, for always having chalk on her nose, and for leading summer "study" trips for students to Europe. In the summer of 1978, Momma scrounged up all of the money she could muster and made it possible for me to join Mrs.

Bennett and several other students on a four-week "study" trip to Spain, Andorra, France and Great Britain.

For a seventeen-year-old small-town boy, that was an intoxicating (no pun intended) experience I couldn't wait to transpire. Four weeks in foreign lands, "studying" in beautiful, historic places I had only seen in the movies, on a globe and in the World Book Encyclopedia.

Our first stop along our journey was Madrid, Spain. Madrid is a beautiful city, and one of the high points of my visit there was touring the Prado, one of the most highly acclaimed museums anywhere. The Prado features paintings, sculptures, prints and drawings by such noted Spanish artists as Goya, Velazquez and El Greco, as well as various art masterpieces from Italy, Belgium, France, Germany, Netherlands and Great Britain. I am not a connoisseur of fine artwork, but I was enthralled with the beauty and elegance of the facility and the treasures that lie within its walls.

Another highlight while in Madrid was attending the bullfights at the Plaza Toros de Madrid on July 2, 1978. We were advised of the high intensity of gore, blood and death we would witness prior to our witnessing the demise of six bulls. Without any hesitancy, the Spanish culturally accept the killing of the bulls by the matador, primarily because the meat derived from the slaughtered animals would be used to feed the poor and homeless. Being teenage kids who had never been away from home very much, and many of us having squeamish tendencies, we devised our own method of coping with the situation.

We would begin drinking sangria, a native drink to Spain consisting of wine, brandy, chopped fruit and sugar. Surely, this would cut the edge off of the gruesomeness we would behold. Drink after drink, we prepared ourselves for the six bulls' ultimate doom. We would consume mass quantities of the sweet beverage, not knowing all the while that, not only was it cutting the edge, it was inebriating all of us, as well.

As we arrived at the bullfight, in our alcohol-compromised state, we learned that an event of historical significance in recent Spanish lore was taking place that afternoon. Soon after he gained power at the end of the Spanish Civil War in 1940 the Spanish dictator, Francisco Franco, outlawed female matadors for "moral" reasons, acting as if he was protecting the safety and femininity of women. His ultimate intent was to disparage the role of women in Spanish society and culture. Franco remained in power until his death in 1975, but the effects of his edict denying female matadors their right to bullfight would remain intact for three more years after his demise.

That fateful Sunday afternoon in July 1978, we would witness a woman matador face not just one, but two bulls in the ring. Maribel Atienzar, at the tender young age of eighteen, would make Spanish history in front of an anxious, excited and adoring legion of Spanish admirers, as well as a few of us Americans and other foreigners scattered among the twenty-five thousand gathered there. Atienzar would become the first woman in over thirty-eight years to fight a bull inside the hallowed ring of Plaza del Toros de Madrid.

As drinking was allowed freely within the confines of the arena, without regard to age, physical or mental state, my friends and I continued our party-hearty ways by chugging sangria from a leather flask that resembled a canteen. To this day, I don't know where the container came from, and who all had been drinking from it before. Teenage ignorance and excitement dictated that we didn't care, particularly since we were already intoxicated by our day-long sangria consumption.

After the opening parade of the three matadors, the bullfight began. The first bull to arrive into the ring appeared to be smaller than what I had anticipated. Of course, my vision may have been impaired by the sangria. The Spanish people rose and roared in unison as their soon-to-be newly-crowned young female national hero entered the ring. Flowers were tossed into the air and into the ring as the tiny, seemingly innocent Maribel Atienzar made her official appearance. We, of course, proudly and vociferously joined them in their revelry.

After the picadors and the banderillos performed their initial acts of tearing into the neck muscles of the bull with spears and planting barbed sticks ordained with paper in the local colors into the bull's spinal area, Atienzar then came out with her cape and sword, intent on facing down the ravaged bull and, ultimately, spearing through the body of the bull and into its aorta. At that very moment, and in our teenage naivety, we didn't understand the significance of all that we were witnessing, only that we looked and felt like Europeans by drinking from a leather flask, and that we were watching the bloody slaying of the bulls.

What we thought were Spanish television cameras were all around the arena covering this momentous event. On one occasion, the cameras focused on us as we reveled in the atmosphere of the bullfight. Not wanting to disappoint our Spanish television admirers, we raised our flask toward the crystal blue Spanish sky in a loud toast to Maribel Atienzar, honoring her for the courage, skill and strength she was displaying that day.

Though I was in a compromised state of mind, I ardently took the memories of the bullfight back to our hotel and still hold them closely to this day. The aftermath of that day's events; well, let's just say that I most definitely, in true Hulsey fashion, was in the wrong place at the wrong time.

Not one of us was feeling very well as we arrived back at our hotel. There was no way of calculating the volume of sangria, together with the sweet, wine and brandy soaked fruits that adorned it, we consumed on that Sunday afternoon. After a few drinks, one loses count. It was still early evening, and we would turn in to bed early, without eating dinner. I spent most of my night hovered over the toilet...the baño, as the Spanish term it. I planned to swear off drinking sangria ever again once that night was over. I haven't so much as sipped any since that day.

As morning arose in Madrid, the aftereffects of the drunken stupor were unpleasant and downright sickening. My head ached, and so did my back and shoulders, having hovered over the toilet most of the night. Somehow gaining entry, Mrs. Bennett charged into our room and immediately began ranting and raving over the condition of the surroundings. Our room was completely in shambles with clothes and trash strewn all over.

She had received complaints from the hotel manager about someone vociferously and intensely praying aloud all night long, swearing to the Good Lord that he would never touch a drop of sangria as long as he lived if the Good Lord would help him through that evening. Of course, that seeker of righteous forgiveness was none other than yours truly. Guests all over the hotel could hear my cries of confession to the Almighty through our open window.

Mrs. Bennett jerked the covers off of the two queen-size beds that had provided a partial night's respite for me and five other guys that prior evening. She proceeded to chastise us for the condition of our room, and for the show I had put on the last evening. She also informed me that I had received a call at the hotel front desk from Momma and Daddy, and that I needed to contact them at once. My first thought was that something wrong may have happened at home, otherwise, why would they be calling me? What on God's green earth could have taken place that created the need to "contact them at once?"

All of a sudden, the groginess and fatigue from a long day and night of partying had now turned to fear and trepidation as I walked the long halls of our Spanish hotel to its main lobby. There, the concierge assisted me as I placed my first-ever international call back home. As an unfamiliar ringtone began to chime through the seemingly antiquated telephone, I could hear a distant, yet sweet voice answer on the other end. It was Momma, and I hadn't heard from her in several days.

It was comforting to have the nurturer of my life's journey to be speaking to me. I greeted Momma with a hearty "hello," and told her about the great time I was already experiencing on my European journey. Momma responded, "That's wonderful, and that's why we called you. I am going to let you speak with your father about that a little more. I'm glad to hear you're okay, son – here's your father." I thought, "Oh no!" Daddy got on the line.

"Son, this is your father. What in the 'Sam Hill' is going on over there?" I was unsure of what Daddy was talking about, so I posed the best question I knew to ask at the time – "huh?" Daddy said, "You know exactly what I'm talking about, boy. Your mother and I were watching the CBS Sunday Evening News on television last night, and they were covering the bullfight in Madrid because the lady matador was fighting. They found it to be an interesting story and of historical significance. And, guess what son, as your mother and I were watching and looking for you in that mass of admirers, lo and behold, the cameras zoomed straight on you. Amazing that, in that large throng of people, they would zero in on you and your friends. Why, it's almost miraculous.

"What was even more unbeleiveable was how much fun you were having, particularly with that large leather flask thrust into your mouth. We sent you over there for a good time, that's true, but not like you were acting at that bullfight. So, either you settle down and get your act together, or we will book you a ticket for home immediately. Do you get what I am saying to you? Am I making myself clear?"

I was utterly schocked and amazed. Thousands of miles away from home, in a time zone six hours ahead of Rockmart, with twenty-five thousand cavorting spectators and who does the CBS News decide to point their cameras on? Well, none other than yours truly, that's who. I thought to myself, "What kind of luck is that?" I thought, "Why me, Lord? Why me?"

Poster purchased at the bullfight in Madrid, Spain.

CHAPTER FOUR:
MY BEST TRIBUTE TO DADDY

After graduating from Rockmart High School in 1979, I headed off to college. Well, let's just say that I attended college and came home every day. I enrolled at Georgia State University (GSU) in Atlanta that, at that time, had no dormitories for the students to live in. That was fine by me, because I wanted to come home each day to my girlfriend and Momma's home cooking.

I would ride to Atlanta each morning with Tim Spencer, who worked near GSU at the Georgia State Capitol at the Department of Education. Tim would pick me up each morning at our house and drop me off right in front of the Urban Life Building at GSU. After classes, I would walk several blocks each day to the Trailways Bus Station, where I would catch the bus home for the 50-mile trek back to Rockmart. Needless to say, that got to be old and tiring very quickly.

I lasted just two semesters at GSU, and then enrolled at Floyd Junior College (now known as Georgia Highlands College) in Rome, Georgia. I decided that I wanted to be a sports writer and that I would pursue that career through my studies. My problem, however, was that I didn't want to study. I was too busy chasing girls and playing spades with my buddies out in the common area of the college. I was still living at home with Momma and Daddy, but Daddy never really spoke to me much during those days.

He was becoming withdrawn for some reason. What was it with him? I could only wonder. Evidently, something was weighing heavily on his mind.

In 1980, I landed a job as a part-time sports writer for the Rome News-Tribune and the Rockmart Journal while still attending Floyd Junior College. A Rockmart native, Orbie Thaxton, was the sports editor for the Rome paper and the editor-in-chief for the Rockmart paper. Orbie was very short in stature, not a midget or a dwarf, but he resembled one. But what he lacked in stature, he made up for it with a warm, caring heart and a zest for life. He was contagious – you wanted to be around Orbie.

Orbie assigned me to cover the Rome-area youth baseball leagues, as well as the local golf tournaments, and the Shorter College Hawks basketball and baseball programs. Man, this was right up my alley, getting to cover all of these sporting events. I just knew that Daddy would be impressed with my sports writing. It would be a while before I would find out how he truly felt.

Orbie would, on occasion, ask me to write a column for the paper. It was always an honor to write a column because I could subject my own thoughts and opinions into what I was writing about. In February of 1981, I was offered the opportunity of writing a column on any subject, dealing with sports, that I desired. Spring training was in full swing in Major League Baseball, so I considered penning a column about baseball dads. I thought it might interest readers to learn more about some of the fathers of the Atlanta Braves players, and how they had inspired their sons throughout their baseball careers.

I only had a couple of days to submit my column. I must have been out of my mind to think I would be able to reach out to any of the Atlanta Braves or their fathers, particularly in such a short time span. And then, like a stroke of lightning, it hit me right there in my little cubicle in the newsroom of the Rome News-Tribune. I would write a column about Daddy. That could be a very early Father's Day gift to him and, maybe, just maybe, it would make him proud of me.

I was only nineteen-years old at the time, but I wanted to speak like a grown man – to a grown man – my father. What a great opportunity I had been afforded, and I had better not mess it up. So, with my thoughts centered on Daddy, I composed this short, simple and heartfelt column:

Rome News-Tribune February 26, 1981 "Special Man – Where Would I Be Without Him" Staff Sportswriter and Columnist Brad Hulsey
Used with permission of Otis Brumby III, Publisher, Times-Journal, Inc.

Over the years, I have had several people help me in so many ways. When it comes to sports, many names come to mind. This column is devoted to one particular man whom I feel I owe the most to.

When I was just a little tot, I saw this man all but break his back working with other kids. Although I wasn't old enough to participate in sports yet, he was constantly toiling at the

60 CENTS

Rockmart Little League Baseball field in Rockmart so that when it came time for me to play, there would be a place and some sort of system to play under.

This man never once has pushed me into doing anything as far as sports is concerned. He merely worked hard so that the opportunity was there for me to do whatever I wanted to do.

He always told me that "the most gratifying thing to see is the smile on your face when you come off that ballfield." This man was not concerned about the awards and recognition that comes with working with kids. He was just happy to be working with us.

Some of his accomplishments over the past two decades in sports include: Rockmart Little League Baseball President, Vice-President, Director and Safety Director; member of the Rockmart Recreation Authority; and, a member and officer of the Rockmart Touchdown Club.

This may not seem like a great deal to some people, but I think it is a great record of service. There are not many men who can work eight hours a day and then come in and devote eight or so more hours in service to the kids of the community.

Now, I know that when he reads this he is going to wonder why in the world I wrote this. The reason is I love this man more than any other man on this earth. I appreciate the things that he has done for me over the years, and I feel that it is high time I showed him how much I do appreciate him.

BRAD HULSEY

If you are wondering who this man that I have been speaking of is, he is my father. I am very proud of him, and I felt like sharing it with everyone. Daddy, thank you for everything you have ever done for me. I am forever indebted to you.

Not exactly a Pulitzer Prize winning column, but it got my message across to Daddy in the best way I knew how – my own words. I was willing to open up and "put myself out there" publicly, so that everyone would know how I felt. As Orbie and the other editors read the column prior to its being submitted for print, each one of them gave me a pat on the back or a hug, stating what a nice gesture it was and how they knew it would be meaningful to so many readers.

All I cared about was what would it mean to Daddy. I wanted him to be proud – proud of me, and proud of himself. I hoped this could bridge a gap that seemed to exist in our relationship. Whatever was going on in his life, I wanted Daddy to know that who he was and what he did mattered. I needed to feel that about myself, too. I could only imagine that it had been difficult for Daddy having lost Granddaddy Hulsey so young in his life, and that he didn't have that father figure in his life to help reassure him as he went about his daily life.

The Rome News-Tribune was delivered to our home on Ivy Street in Rockmart daily. That Thursday afternoon, February 26, 1981, I arrived home after a long day of school and sports writing. Daddy was waiting on the front porch. In his hand, he held the sports section of the Rome News-Tribune. His lips were quivering, and I could see on his cheeks tears flowing like a misty rainfall.

As I ascended the steep flight of steps that led to our front porch there on Ivy Street, Daddy grabbed me and hugged me like he had never before. All was right between my Daddy and me at that time. He kept thanking me for the column, and told me how much it meant to him. Anything that had gotten in the way of our being father and son retreated for those few precious moments. It was a special time between father and son, and a rare occasion for Daddy and me.

CHAPTER FIVE:
POLITICS

Daddy had never shown an interest in politics; however, he did always vote during every election. I can remember his being a Richard Nixon fan during the 1968 Presidential election, but I couldn't recall his being a political pundit or one who would seek office. All of that changed in the fall of 1979, when he was asked to consider running for the Rockmart City Council Ward 3 post.

Daddy had no clue about running for political office, but I did – well, at least I knew about running for a position. After all, I had been Sophomore Class Vice-President, and Junior and Senior Class President of Rockmart High School. Even before that, I was elected President of Mrs. Helen Sproull's second grade class at Goodyear Elementary School in 1968. So, I considered myself a seasoned public servant.

Daddy would be facing two other Rockmart gentlemen who had never held public office, Riley Evans and Gene Sorrells. He asked me to be his campaign manager, a great honor for a son and a young teenage man. I helped draft speeches, campaign newspaper ads, mailout materials and signage. I helped Daddy canvas the Ward in which he was seeking to serve, and I got to meet a lot of interesting "Rockmartians" along the way.

Daddy and Riley Evans wound up in a runoff election, and

Daddy eventually won the seat. I was so proud of him. Yet another community activity that Daddy would become involved in.

Daddy had been very active in so many areas in the community, including his various positions with the Rockmart Little League, as a Board Member of the Rockmart-Aragon Hospital Authority, a Board Member of the Rockmart Recreation Authority, President of the Rockmart Jaycees, Director of the Rockmart Touchdown Club, and, now, City Councilman. Quite the resume, to say the least.

Oddly enough, during the entire campaign for City Council, there was never any discussion or questions raised about Daddy's Hulsey heritage, nor about Granddaddy Hulsey, who had died when Daddy was such a small lad and left him fatherless. Nothing ever came up regarding William Robert, who died at such an early age, or Marion, who was stillborn. Typical politicians use those types of stories to make a sympathetic connection with the voters.

Many years later, Joe Biden used the sad and untimely deaths of his wife and daughter in a tragic automobile accident one week before Christmas 1972 in a meaningful and powerful way during his selection as Barack Obama's vice-presidential running mate back in 2008 (for the record, I voted for John McCain). I guess the family lineage and history wasn't important in a local race for city council. Those types of issues were only talked about within the family, if at all, or by others, in private and in secret.

I asked Daddy one day why he was so involved in the community. Although I didn't want him to know, it really bothered me that he was so busy doing for others that he didn't have more time for his family. Daddy told me that the Rockmart community had been so good to him his entire life, from the time he was a small child until the present, and that he wanted to give back more than he had received.

Daddy then told me something that has stuck with me my entire life, and that has framed me as a person in all that I do. He said to me, "Son, there are those whose purpose in life is to serve others, and to serve their community. Right here, right now at this time, I am telling you that is your purpose, and don't you ever forget it." That was the most profound statement Daddy ever made to me, one that has driven me to do so many things in my life. It sticks to me like glue, and permeates my inner being like a nail being driven through a wooden beam.

After having won reelection to a second two-year term on the Rockmart City Council, and having neared the end of that second term in 1982, Daddy was forced to not seek reelection for a third term, at least not for one year. The U.S. Department of Justice required the City of Rockmart to redistrict their five city wards, based upon the Federal Voting Rights Act of 1965. The Act called for an equal balance of the number of voters in any political jurisdiction (in Rockmart's case – wards), as well as an appropriately balanced ratio of minority voters in each ward.

Under the redistricting plan, our residence and all of Ivy

Street would be redistricted out of Ward 3 and into Ward 2. Dr. John Atha, a nine-year veteran on the city council and one of the more well-respected men in town, held the Ward 2 council post. He had one year remaining in his term. Daddy would either have to uproot and move us all into another ward in the city, or he would have to sit this election out. Wisely, he chose the latter and, at least for then, his political days were over. We would soon learn that it was for the best.

In 1983, after having been redistricted out of an opportunity to seek reelection for his Ward 3 council post, Daddy began contemplating a run for John Atha's Ward 2 position. Rumor had it that Dr. Atha had decided that he might not seek another two-year term, as he was in the final months of his fifth term and tenth year total. Daddy had enjoyed serving the citizens of Rockmart and, with Dr. Atha potentially backing out, the door was opening for another opportunity to serve.

Daddy had been feeling somewhat nauseated for several days, and he noticed a small amount of blood in his stool when he would use the restroom. He didn't pay much attention to this, and simply treated himself for an on again-off again case of hemorrhoids. After several weeks of continual bleeding, constipation and cramping, Daddy decided it was time to have Dr. Charlie Smith (the same doctor who had delivered me over twenty-one years prior and for whom Momma was still working) to take a close look at what was going on.

After several examinations, x-rays and tests, both in

Rockmart and in Rome at Redmond Regional Medical Center, the news wasn't good. Daddy was diagnosed with colorectal cancer. We were all devastated, particularly Daddy. It brought to my mind the day Barry Owen and I had walked all over Ivy Street, knocking on every door for our ill-gotten gain for the "Kansur Society". Now, cancer was for real in our lives, particularly Daddy's. He was only fifty-nine years old, and he was about to be in the toughest battle of his life. Well, at least the toughest physical battle of his life.

Daddy began radiation treatments at the oncologist's offices in Rome. He would go back and forth for daily treatments for several weeks. My uncle, Willie Hardy, the husband of Momma's only sister, Aunt Dossie (as we affectionately call her, her given name being Doris), was a Godsend for Momma and Daddy, driving Daddy the forty-plus mile round trip each day to and from his treatments. Once the tumor inside his rectum had shrunk enough for surgery, the physicians determined, with Daddy's blessings, that a colostomy was the best alternative to rid his body of the cancer that was eating away at him.

The colostomy was performed, successfully (if that isn't an oxymoron). After all, how could sewing your rear end up and, after removing a section of your colon and then rerouting the colon through an incision on your side near your rib cage so that you could uncontrollably poop into a bag that you had to change on a frequent basis daily be success? On top of all of that, once he had "recuperated" from his surgery, Daddy would have to endure even more radiation treatments. Those radiation treatments burned his bottom so badly that he would literally sit in a basin of cold water for hours, soaking his parched rear end.

Daddy was in no shape to work anymore. The wear and tear of the cancer and subsequent treatments he was enduring were too much for him to bear, along with holding down a full-time job. For Goodyear's part, after having been employed for forty-one years, they graciously granted Daddy permanent medical disability status and, thus, ended his career with Goodyear.

Goodyear had always been good to its employees, and this was just another example of their care of those who helped make their company so successful. After forty-one years, it pained Daddy to have to say goodbye to all of his co-workers, and so many memories. Also, Daddy couldn't consider a run for City Council again.

Although Dr. Atha was still "hinting" that he would not seek another term, it just wasn't in the cards for Daddy that year. I thought, if it were at all possible, it would be good for Daddy to serve on the city council once more. It would keep him busy, he would have more time to devote to his duties, and he was all about serving his community. But, it wasn't possible. Daddy was too weak from the cancer treatments and colostomy.

And then, I remembered what Daddy had said to me. At that moment, Daddy's words struck a chord with me like the tune to "Amazing Grace", one that I can recall at the snap of a finger. I remembered his emphatically saying to me, "Son, there are those whose purpose in life is to serve others, and to serve their community. Right here, right now at this time, I am telling you that is your purpose, and don't you ever forget it."

Since Daddy couldn't do it, well, it was my time. I was going to run for city council in Rockmart. I couldn't wait to tell Daddy, and when I did, his reply hit me like a ton of bricks. "Oh no, Son...don't even think about it. Yes, you're old enough and, yes, you're a registered voter. You aren't a convicted felon, even though you've done some crazy and mischievous things in your twenty-one years of existence. You're not even a taxpayer, or a property owner. You still live at home with me and your Momma. And, what if, think about it, what if John Atha changes his mind and decides to run again?"

****

It was early in October of 1983, and qualifying for city council and mayor would be held on Tuesday, October 18th. I had heard what Daddy said about my running for city council. Would I listen to his words then and not qualify, or those words he spoke to me three years prior about my serving the community?

Momma and Daddy had been invited by Dr. Charlie Smith and his wife, Julaine, to join them for a week-long trip to their mountain home in Highlands, North Carolina. They headed out that Sunday morning, October 16th, with hopes that Daddy could get some much-needed rest, and so that Momma could, too, having been Daddy's caretaker at home and working full-time for Dr. Smith. They were both worn out.

When qualifying day rolled around, I was chomping at the bit to run for city council. I knew that if Dr. Atha didn't seek reelection, I would have a chance at "serving others and serving the community" as Daddy had prescribed for me. Against Daddy's advice, I filled out my qualifications papers and paid the whopping $18.00 qualifying fee. I was running for the Ward 2 City Council post in Rockmart! No one else had qualified at that time, so I was cautiously optimistic that, perhaps, I would "walk in" unopposed. That would not be the case.

Dr. Atha had a change in heart, stating that, after ten years of service, there still was some unfinished business he hoped to take care of. I thought "Oh my goodness! I've got to run against a ten-year incumbent, a man who had delivered many of Rockmart's babies, whose son Ben and I had been lifelong friends (and continue to be to this day), and who has given so much to this community." What was I thinking? Well, I was thinking that Dr. Atha wasn't going to run again, of course. So much for that thought.

I then thought back to my childhood, and what Ms. Elizabeth Carter had said to Phil and me many, many years ago, "You boys aren't nothing but old Hulseys," she exclaimed. I was determined to show that ornery old lady what this "old Hulsey" could accomplish.

Momma and Daddy arrived home that Saturday from their mountain getaway, seeming fresh and renewed. That was good for me, since I wanted them, particularly Daddy, in a good mood when I broke the news of my qualifying to run for city council to them. As we were outside unloading the luggage from the car, without hesitation Daddy blurted out to me, "So, where did you get the $18.00 to qualify?" I was caught off guard. How had he found out? It wasn't as if my qualifying would have made the Highlands, N.C. newspapers or local television news. Someone must have called Daddy and told him.

I sheepishly asked him, "Daddy, how did you find out?" "I didn't find out, Son," he replied. "I just knew when we left here last weekend that you were going to qualify and run for city council. I assume you used your own money to pay your qualifying fee. That's good. It shows you're in this for the right reasons and that you're willing to put your money where your mouth is. So, what about John Atha? Is he running, too? How about anyone else, since the qualifying period has closed? Is anyone else running?"

I thought, "Wow, Daddy is actually talking to me about this, and he doesn't appear to be angry with me." I began to rant, "Well, Daddy, yes sir, you see, Dr. Atha wasn't going to run, and so I qualified knowing that, and all of a sudden, I hear he did qualify, and, well, I've stepped into a big pile of you-know-what here, Daddy."

Daddy smiled, put his arms around my shoulders and pulled me up close to him, having me to squat down to look directly through his bifocals and into his eyes. Looking directly at me, his voice quivering with a multitude of emotions onboard, Daddy said, "It's my fault you're in this.

60 CENTS

I told you a few years ago it was your purpose to serve others and to serve your community. That's what you're attempting to do. Now, go – and, WIN!" That was all I needed to hear from my father.

The election was held on Saturday, December 3, 1983. Between qualifying and election day, I would knock on each and every door in Ward 2. It was heartwarming to me how friendly and open the people of Rockmart were.

Even though I was so young, and really had no clue of what I was talking about, I took time to go into citizen's homes, to sit down in their living rooms, to enjoy a piece of cake at their tables. What I lacked in knowledge, I made up for by listening, and taking notes. I did every bit of it on my own.

Daddy wasn't physically able to campaign with me, but he did write me a $25.00 check to help with my expenses. That meant so much to me. I even went to the Atha's residence, knowing that they weren't going to support me. I spoke with Dr. Atha and, as I would have expected, he treated me like a gentleman and was very thoughtful, even though I was his opponent. I will always respect him for the class he showed this young man that day.

During the door-to-door campaign, there were two homes I would visit that, based on the outcome of those visits, would forever impact me personally. Both former Mayor Fred Braswell, and current Mayor George Harvey "Red" Scott lived in Ward 2. Mayor Scott was finishing his fifth term (ten years total) as Rockmart's mayor. He had entered office at the same time Dr. Atha did, so there was a ten-year history and working relationship between the two gentlemen. Former Mayor Braswell had been out of office for nearly sixteen years, but was still heavily involved in the community. His first wife, Martha Jane Braswell, had passed away back in 1980. By now, he had remarried a charming lady by the name of Jewell Sproull Hall, and had moved into another area of Ward 2 into his new bride's home.

My meeting with Fred Braswell wasn't very long. As we talked, he shared his admiration for both Dr. Atha and me. He recalled the days of Phil and me playing all over the neighborhood and in his front yard. He bowed his head in shame, and offered an apology. "Brad, I am so sorry for how Ms. Elizabeth Carter treated you and your brother years ago. I swear, that was not of me, I hope you know. But I am truly, truly sorry, and I am truly sorry for all the pain your daddy has endured over the many years."

He wouldn't commit to me whether or not he would be voting for me, but his words meant more to me than any vote could have. Apology accepted on my behalf, but there was also confusion that set in. What did Fred Braswell mean when he said, "and I am truly sorry for all the pain your Daddy has endured over the many years?" It hadn't been "many years" since Daddy had been diagnosed with cancer. And, how, if any way, did his comment parallel with the "old Hulseys" statement our malcontent neighbor, Ms. Elizabeth Carter, had called Phil and me years ago? I had to wonder. Those old secrets keep coming back up, whatever they are – or aren't.

The last visit I would have prior to Election Day was at the home of Mayor Red Scott and his lovely wife, Clara Head Scott. I had known both of them for my entire life. Red was the former President of the Rockmart Bank, and Clara was still working at the bank at that time. Red had been a very effective leader as Mayor, having directed the town through difficult financial times during the late 1970s and in forging relationships with state and local officials in positive and proactive economic development efforts.

When I arrived at the Scott home that Friday afternoon prior to Saturday's election, Clara met me at the door with her sweet smile and a warm hug. I was shaking like a leaf with nervousness as I awaited the verdict from Red. I just knew that he would be voting for Dr. Atha, since they had "unfinished business" that Dr. Atha had talked about, and that Red would need for Dr. Atha to see their unfinished efforts through to the end, since Red wasn't seeking reelection. Clara escorted me to a room in the back of their lovely, quaint home there on South Depot Street in Rockmart.

Red was seated with his trademark unlit cigar in his right cheek, swaying back and forth in a small rocking chair that creaked loudly with each forward and backward thrust. He asked me to take a seat across from him in a straight chair, and he politely excused Clara. And then, the Mayor spoke, "Brad, I've known you all of your life. I've known your Momma and Daddy for practically all of their lives. There are probably things that I know that you don't have a clue about, but that doesn't matter right now.

"I've been serving with John Atha for ten years down there at City Hall. John is a good man, and he's done a good job on the council. He's supported me on most everything. Anyhow, Clara and I have done a lot of talking."

Red stopped for a moment to take his cigar out of his mouth, and he ceased rocking. The room became eerily quiet as Red leaned forward, his breath smelling like unsmoked tobacco from the cigar.

"Brad, Clara and I admire the fact that a young person wants to be involved in our city government. I'm sure you learned plenty from your daddy over the years. We're crazy about John, but we believe it's time for some young folks to take over the reins. I just wanted to tell you in person that Clara and I will be voting for you tomorrow."

I nearly fell over with joy. I couldn't believe what my ears were hearing. The Mayor and the First Lady of Rockmart will be voting for me, a twenty-two-year- old political novice who was only doing what his father couldn't do due to health. I was simply attempting to serve others and my community, just like Daddy said. I didn't feel I had much of a chance to defeat Dr. Atha but, by golly, I had given it my best effort. And the Mayor would be voting for me – WOW!

The day dawned on Election Day, and it was a rainy mess. The temperature wasn't too cold, but the rain made for a miserable day to get out to vote. I had coffee that morning at the Yellow Jacket Café, courtesy of Pete and Ronnie Huckeba, my old neighbors on Ivy Street and staunch supporters of my campaign. Citywide voting took place at the Senior Citizens Center that was located adjacent to the Community Theater on Elm Street in downtown Rockmart.

There was also voting that day for the mayor's seat, as well as other council positions. I stood out in the rain across the street from the polling area, shaking hands with anyone I could come in contact with. I held an umbrella over my head, but I still got wet. My body may have been dampened, but my spirits were not. I didn't expect to win, but the campaign had been a time of growth, renewal and joy for me.

A few hours before the polls closed, having stood in the rain all day by myself, I saw Daddy's car pull into the municipal parking lot. He came over and said hello, and then he went in to the polling place to vote. I noticed how small and frail he looked, worn down by the cancer surgery and treatments. But he was there to vote for me, and I couldn't have been more grateful.

When Daddy departed the polling area, I anticipated he would come over just to say goodbye. Instead, he opened up his own umbrella, and stood with me for an hour in the pouring down rain, supporting his son. After all, it was "his fault" that I was running anyway, so I thought. It made me smile to have him stand next to me in that place, at that time.

When the polls closed, I went into the polling area. Daddy had already gone home to be with Momma. I was there with many of the other candidates, except Dr. Atha. I supposed that he had been through many of these, and that he was rightfully confident that he would be declared the victor. When all of the votes had been tallied, I couldn't believe my eyes! I had won, and rather convincingly, with 63% of the votes.

I had done it. I had won an election, and in the process, I just knew that I had made my Daddy proud because, now, I had a great opportunity to serve others, and to serve my community. I ran home to tell Momma and Daddy, and they were elated. Daddy and I cried tears of joy together. I wanted to tell the world, and I wanted Ms. Elizabeth Carter to know that another "old Hulsey" had overcome whatever that meant to do something extraordinary.

I soon learned that I was (and still am) the youngest elected official in Rockmart history. I would go on to serve seven years on the City Council in Rockmart along with a great mentor and friend of mine and a superb leader, Steven B. Smith, who was elected to his first of several terms as Rockmart's Mayor, replacing "Red" Scott.

I was honored to serve with Rockmart's first elected black city official, Sandy McClure, on the City Council, as well as with several other outstanding servant leaders and City Council Members that included Orbie Thaxton, Nathan "Yank" Schmeck, Riley Evans, Jack Quick, Chuck Pinkard, Bobby Helms, Scott Kinney, Steve Holder, and the first-elected female city official, Sharon Baulding.

For his part, John Atha would go on to distinguish himself by serving the citizens of Rockmart and Polk County as an elected member of the Polk County School Board. When I would call on him for help and guidance, Dr. Atha would gladly offer sage advice to me on City matters, being the admirable man he always was.

Later on in my life, I would have the privilege of serving four years on the City Council in Powder Springs, Georgia, and four years as Mayor of Powder Springs, all in the name of serving others and serving community. But that record of being the youngest elected official in the history of my hometown of Rockmart is something I will always cherish.

Hulsey wins...

Dec. 7, 1983

Brackett, Smith facing runoff for mayor's post

Despite bad weather, over 60 percent of the registered voters in Rockmart turned out to vote in the 1983 elections, but failed to decide a winner and now must return to the polls on Dec. 17th to determine the new mayor for the City of Rockmart.

Rockmart Councilman Steven (Steve) Smith led the ticket of four candidates with 39 percent of the votes, while former City manager Ronald Brackett finished with 26 percent – forcing the runoff.

Meanwhile, the only council seat with opposition proved to be an upset win for 22-year-old Brad Hulsey, son of former Councilman Fred Hulsey, as he defeated incumbent John Atha, 113-59 for the Ward 2 post.

Incumbent Councilman Nathan (Yank) Schmeck was returned to office without opposition. He received a total of 140 votes from Ward 5 voters.

Meanwhile, in the Aragon elections, John C. (Jake) Belk was elected without opposition as mayor replacing Larry Pittman.

In the council races, two political newcomers walked off with the two open berths. Dewey Ward led the ticket of six with 93 votes, while Woodrow Brumbelow was second with 89 votes. Others in the race included Doug Rayburn with 24 votes, John R. Podskoc with 22, Ricky Taylor with 20 and Bill Craton with eight.

A total of 253 people are registered in Aragon and 134 votes were cast or 52.9 percent. Six ballots were void.

The winners will take office in January, replacing Councilmen Podskoc and Belk. They'll join Eugene Smith and William (Buddy) Tanner on the Aragon Council.

In the Rockmart Mayoral race, Smith finished with 309 votes or 39 percent, while Brackett had 200 or 26 percent. Ronnie Hutcheson had 156 votes or 20 percent and Donald Gurley finished with 115 votes of 15 percent.

Smith, who has served on the Council for nine years, was high voter getter in each of the machines, receiving 168 in the non-council wards, 75 in Ward 2 and 54 in Ward 5. He also received 12 absentee votes. Brackett was second with 115 in non-council wards, while finishing third in Ward 5 with 35. He had five absentee votes. Hutcheson won second place in the Ward 5 balloting.

Thus, Smith and Brackett will faceoff in a runoff on December 17th with all registered voters eligible to vote.

COUNCILMAN-ELECT BRAD HULSEY
Father, Fred, congratulates winner

Article from *The Rockmart Journal* proclaiming my victory. (Used with permission of Otis Brumby III, Publisher, Times-Journal Inc.)

CHAPTER SIX:
THE HALL OF FAME

In 1985, having already gone through the surgery for his colostomy, and experiencing the insufferable ordeal of dealing with the radiation and subsequent chemotherapy treatments, Daddy's colorectal cancer had metastasized to his right lung. He was at the lowest of lows, and so were we, his family who loved and cared for him. Once again, surgery and chemotherapy were needed to treat Daddy's cancer-ridden body.

The colostomy had been performed in Rome, Georgia, at Redmond Regional Medical Center. The lung surgery would take place in Atlanta at Georgia Baptist Hospital. A portion of Daddy's lung needed to be removed to hopefully remove all of the cancer. After the surgery, additional chemotherapy treatment was prescribed to make certain that all of the cancer cells would be eliminated.

Daddy got through the lung surgery fairly well, and handled the chemotherapy like the trooper he always was. But the cancer, the colostomy, and all of the treatments were taking a toll on his body. He wouldn't allow it all to take away his spirit and determination, however. Yes, he was on permanent medical disability, and he faced more chemotherapy. That did not stop Daddy from pulling himself up by his bootstraps and going about a new-normal way of living.

He was stubborn as an old mule, and I watched him with

wonder and amazement as he would work for hours in the garden he had planted in our back yard, replete with tomatoes, cucumbers, squash, peppers, okra, eggplant and other vegetarian delights. Daddy had a green thumb, and it showed in his garden. He tilled up good ole red Georgia clay, cultivated the soil, planted, fertilized, watered and grew a masterpiece of a garden. The garden work and the cancer treatments took a toll on Daddy, too.

The emotions I felt would grow more intense one day when, watching from a distance, I saw Daddy turn his head away from his garden and then begin to vomit profusely in the adjacent grass under the clothesline in the back yard. His body was imperfect, but Daddy faced the demon of cancer head-on, with determination and reckless abandon, just like he had on the football field some forty years previously.

Daddy would have run right through the cancer if he could have, just like he had run the eighty-yard punt return for a touchdown against the Cedartown Bulldogs, marching toward ultimate victory. We would all soon learn that final and ultimate victory would come in a very different form than we had hoped and prayed for.

The cancer that had eaten away at Daddy's colorectal system and his lung had now spread to his liver. The doctors didn't give much encouragement, except to suggest additional chemotherapy and a whole lot of prayer. The tumor that had formed on Daddy's liver was so large that it was pushing his liver against the diaphragm of his stomach. Consequently, this caused day-long, non-stop hiccups and severe vomiting of bile. It made it very difficult for him to eat, and he began to shrivel down to a mere impression of the man he used to be. Daddy faced the giant of liver cancer just like David faced Goliath, but he knew that the story would not have the same ending for him as it did for David as he slew the giant.

****

Rockmart is located in Polk County, Georgia, the 48th most populated county of the 159 counties in Georgia. There are three incorporated cities in Polk County. Cedartown is the county seat, and then there is Rockmart and Aragon. There are several smaller communities in the unincorporated areas of the county, including a small section known as Van Wert.

In the 1970s and 1980s, the Polk County Chamber of Commerce held an awards banquet each year at which time they would bestow honors upon the Man and Woman of the Year for Rockmart, as well as the installation of a deserving citizen into the Rockmart Hall of Fame. Many of Rockmart's distinguished persons had been enshrined into the Hall of Fame.

One day in 1986, Momma received a phone call from the Chamber of Commerce to inform her that Daddy had been voted into the Rockmart Hall of Fame, and that he would be enshrined and receiving a plaque later that year. It all had to be kept a secret from Daddy and, of course, it was in our blood to be able to keep a good secret for a long time.

Momma had to tell Daddy a "little white lie" in order to get him to attend the banquet. The liver cancer was progressing, in spite of the chemotherapy treatments. The hiccups were not letting up, and the vomiting and weight loss were taking a toll on Daddy's quality of life. Most of his clothes no longer fit him, and he certainly didn't want to wear a suit and tie, particularly a suit that was several sizes too large for him now. Much of his hair had fallen out due to the effects of the chemotherapy treatments.

Daddy would only go to the banquet for one reason, and that was what Momma used in her "little white lie" to get him there. She told Daddy that I was being named Rockmart's Man of the Year for 1986.

Daddy was so proud of me, and he couldn't wait to put on that oversized suit and clip-on tie in order to share in the celebration of his youngest son. Little did he know that in just a few hours, he would become a member of Rockmart's Hall of Fame, honoring him for his work with the Little League, the Touchdown Club, the City Council, Hospital Board, Recreation Authority, Jaycees, Boy Scouts, Rockmart First Baptist Church, and the many other community-based organizations and volunteer efforts he so freely gave of himself to. This would be a culminating evening of all that Fred Avery Hulsey Jr. had done to make his community a better place for his family and so many more to live, work, play and worship.

This was Daddy's night to shine, and for the Hulsey name to be placed in a historic light for the Rockmart community. Little did I know that the Hulsey name had historical significance already, well beyond that of Daddy's accomplishments or my being the youngest city council-man in the City's history. That night, I would get a very tiny, miniscule glimpse into the secret that Daddy and so many held close to.

The banquet was held at the Nathan Dean Community Center on Goodyear Avenue in Rockmart. After dinner and a few remarks from local dignitaries and Chamber leadership, the awards ceremony began. First up was the awarding of Rockmart's Woman of the Year. Ann Arnold, the local development authority chair who did a lot to help redevelop Rockmart's downtown area, deservingly was bestowed that honor.

It came time for the Man of the Year Award to be handed out. You could see the great anticipation in Daddy's eyes as the plaque was being brought out. He was proud of his son, and nothing would keep him away from celebrating that evening with me.

Daddy gazed at Momma with a perplexed and sad face when it was announced that a local developer and longtime Rockmart resident, Freddie Lewis, was named Man of the Year. Had there been a mistake, even though Freddie was a deserving recipient? I know Daddy had to wonder what was going on, and why he had dragged his tired, sick and worn body out to see someone other than his son receive the award. He said nothing to me as the award was being presented to Freddie, but I could see the disappointment for me in his eyes.

The time had arrived for the Hall of Fame award to be

presented. Cliff McCarson, a longtime friend and coworker of Daddy's at Goodyear and a board member of the local Chamber of Commerce, was asked to present the award.

As Cliff began his speech, he spoke of Daddy's courage in the face of adversity, and how he had overcome much in his life as he served the community and his fellow man. He talked of Daddy's devotion to his family, his friends, to the "least of the least", and to the youth of the community. He listed many of Daddy's accomplishments and areas of service where he had committed so much of his life.

I looked at Daddy as Cliff was speaking, and tears were welling up in his eyes. He looked at Momma, pointed his finger at her and said, "Well, I guess you fooled me!" Everyone in the Center knew who Cliff was speaking of, but when Cliff announced Daddy's name as the Hall of Fame recipient for 1986, everyone stood and applauded as Daddy walked to the front to accept his award. I cried like a little baby – I was so proud of my father. Momma, Phil, and the majority of the crowd had tears streaming down their cheeks, as well. We all knew that Daddy's days on earth were few, but that at that very moment, he was larger than life.

As he accepted the award from Cliff and addressed the crowd, Daddy thanked the Chamber of Commerce for thinking of him, and for the honor being bestowed upon him. He thanked Momma and jovially scolded her at the same time for fooling him into being there. Through constant hiccups and a few more tears, Daddy then uttered words that sent my mind into a whirlwind of curiosity and wonderment as I pondered and processed what he was saying:

"Since I was a little boy growing up here in Rockmart, many of you and those who have passed on have contributed a lot to my life. At times, it wasn't easy growing up here and raising my own family, but I did it. I just want to thank everyone who saw fit to help me through the years, even when it might not have been so easy for them or you to do so. Thank you all!"

Daddy then walked away to yet another standing ovation, receiving hugs, kisses, handshakes and pats on the back as he made his way to us, his family. I wondered what Daddy was talking about in his acceptance speech. What did he mean by it all, and what had occurred over the years that stirred his words to his admirers that night? Would I ever find out? Or, would it all be kept a secret?

It was wintertime, and cold and dreary outside. We knew Daddy was entering the twilight season of his life and that, barring a miracle, which we fervently prayed for and believed in, he would be leaving us soon. To have had the opportunity to see Daddy receive the Hall of Fame Award was such an honor and blessing for us, his family. We were so glad he held on long enough to receive the award.

The liver cancer was a force to be reckoned with, and the chemotherapy treatments that Daddy had been taking were stopped by his oncologist. No need to put Daddy through the anguish that the chemicals were pouring through his body. Daddy knew his time was up, as did

Momma, Phil and I. As 1987 rolled around, Daddy would be in and out of the hospital for various associated cancerous complications that would wreak more havoc on his body and his quality of life.

****

On many Saturday afternoons, even before his first cancer diagnosis, Daddy frequented a place he dubbed the "ERBC" in Rome, Georgia. The true identity of this spot was a liquor store located in East Rome that, at that time, was the closest "legal" liquor store to Rockmart. There were various and sundry locations in and around Rockmart where "illegal" distilled spirits could be purchased. Most of the locals knew where those locations existed. Daddy didn't want to harm his reputation by frequenting those particular establishments.

Daddy was resolute in remaining on the up-and-up with his purchases of the hard stuff. His elixir of choice was an 80 proof vodka and one of the cheapest firewaters on the market. He had been partaking of this clear-colored booze for many years, mixing it with grapefruit juice into a concoction he called a "toddy." Most alcoholic beverage aficionados know this drink to be a "greyhound." But that didn't make any difference to Daddy – he just enjoyed his daily toddy.

As Daddy's cancer progressed and his health declined, his mental state began to deteriorate, as well. His visits to the "ERBC" for purchases of the cheap vodka became more and more recurrent. Mixing the toddy with his pain medications and other prescriptions he was taking wasn't safe, and it sometimes caused fits of anger. His fury would be aimed particularly toward the one person he was supposed to love and cherish more than anyone on earth – Momma. I vividly recall how Daddy, after having consumed a few toddies would, for no apparent reason, shout out at Momma in a fit of rage. Usually, she would be brought to tears.

Phil had already moved out of our house and was living in his own home by now, so I felt it was my responsibility to protect Momma and take up for her when Daddy was acting so malicious toward her. Many times, I would verbally confront Daddy about his coldhearted and harsh actions toward Momma. He would come at me with as much vitriol as he would toward Momma, sometimes causing me to weep, as well.

As Daddy's drinking became more and more frequent, I became exasperated at his actions. Yes, I knew he was dealing with the loathsome and debilitating disease of cancer. His body had been terrorized by three years of dealing with three different malignancies. I couldn't understand why he would allow himself to be dredged down into the deep, dark depths of depression and woe, and how he could treat Momma in such a poor and senseless manner.

As far as I was concerned, this was the strongest and toughest guy I knew. A star athlete, a Marine, my father, always on the top of the totem pole when it came to being a "manly man," as far as I was concerned. And now, he had lowered his standards to the point of being an angry, frequent drunkard, one who depended on the bottle to help take away all of his fears and concerns. My respect for Daddy began to wither.

I grilled Momma as to what she thought we should do about Daddy's drinking issues. Momma emphatically told me, "Mind your own business, Son! Your father has had to deal with much more than this cancer over his lifetime, and you don't need to concern yourself with your father's calamities. You take care of yourself, and I'll take care of him!" I had no clue what Momma was talking about. On numerous occasions I had stepped in to protect her from Daddy's fits of rage, and this is how she thanks me? Was Daddy's drinking not just about overcoming his declining health? What more was driving Daddy to consume more and more "toddies"?

****

On Sunday morning, March 8, 1987, Daddy walked out of our home on Ivy Street in Rockmart, only a hint of the man he used to be. His body was frail, worn by the cancer and subsequent treatments. His clothes hung off of his small frame as he gingerly strode to the car. Momma was driving him to Floyd Medical Center, a hospital in Rome, Georgia, in hopes that they could help alleviate some of the pain that the liver tumor was ravishing on his body. The oncologist ordered a morphine drip for Daddy. We all prayed it would stop some of the bodily pain he was experiencing.

Momma would stay with Daddy all of the day Sunday and

into Monday morning. She would sleep in a chair next to his bed.

As he lay in his hospital bed, Daddy sensed a calm come over his body. The morphine was helping with the pain, and it was easing the fighting inner-spirit he had displayed for three-plus years of battling the terrible disease.

I would arrive at the hospital early that afternoon. Momma was completely worn out. I pleaded with her to go home for a few hours to sleep. The hospital was thirty minutes from the house, so she could drive home, sleep a few hours, bathe, grab some clothes and come back. She reluctantly agreed.

I hadn't eaten all day, and I was beginning to get hungry. The cafeteria at Floyd Medical Center was closed for a couple of hours to prepare for dinner. I found a vending machine, purchased a bag of microwave popcorn and popped it up. When I went back into Daddy's room, almost without taking a breath, I consumed most of the popcorn. Daddy was in and out of sleep, and his moaning with pain had subsided.

I asked him if he wanted a small piece of popcorn, and he nodded his head up and down. I knew he couldn't resist the smell. Just like when we used to walk into Allen's 5 and Ten Cents store in downtown Rockmart many years ago, the smell of the fresh-popped popcorn would stir your senses and cause you to purchase a bag or two. I took a kernel of the popcorn and broke off a small piece. I placed it on Daddy's lip and told him to enjoy it. I left the room to return to the vending machine to purchase a soft drink (a Cocola, as we called it). When I returned to Daddy's room, the piece of popcorn was still on his lip, and Daddy was fast asleep.

When the doctor came by to make his final visit of the day, he told me that Daddy was not only asleep, he was semi-comatose. The doctor indicated that it was highly probable that Daddy would never wake up again, and that his body would begin to "shut down". I called Momma at home and urged her to return to the hospital immediately. Momma, Phil and I would keep vigil for the next two days. Many visitors came by to offer their support, knowing that the end was inevitable for Daddy.

Aunt Dossie and Uncle Willie were mainstays, coming and going as they could during those two days. Aunt Hope, Daddy's one living sibling, would visit, bringing Daddy's mother, Maw Maw Vert, with her. Having been a nurse for her entire adult life, Aunt Hope would do little things for Daddy that none of us could do as effectively, like swabbing his lips with ice, adjusting his catheter and oxygen mask. She showed loving care and attention to her big brother.

On Wednesday evening, March 11, 1987 the weather report was calling for snow showers in the Rome-Rockmart area. We always seemed to get snow toward the end of winter; certainly, not at Christmastime. Daddy was still in his semi-comatose state. Momma, Phil and I were totally exhausted from keeping vigil for such a long time. Aunt Dossie and Uncle Willie made their daily visit, just as they had done so many times before when Daddy was hospitalized.

Upon arriving at the Floyd Medical Center, Aunt Dossie's goal was to get Momma to leave the hospital for a while, just to give her a little bit of sanity. She tried to get Momma to go to a restaurant with them, but Momma wasn't having anything to do with that. She didn't want to leave Daddy's side.

Finally, Aunt Dossie convinced Momma to go down to the cafeteria for a cup of coffee. Uncle Willie would stay in Daddy's room with him as Phil and I would be across the hallway in a waiting room.

After thirty minutes or so had passed, Uncle Willie called for Phil and me to come quickly into Daddy's room. As we entered, I could see that Uncle Willie had a look of concern as he gazed down at Daddy's frail body. Daddy's breathing was very shallow, and the heart monitor showed a very low blood pressure and nearly a flat line for the heartbeat. Momma and Aunt Dossie had just gotten back from their much-needed break and quickly moved into the room with us.

Daddy had fought the good fight, but he could no longer hang on. As he breathed his final breaths, I was amazed at how peaceful his death was. Here my earthly father was moving on to be with our Heavenly Father, and I could sense that, while it was a very sad time, Daddy would no longer have to suffer the effects from the menace of cancer. His body would be made whole again.

60 CENTS

Momma stood over Daddy, looking lovingly at the man she had been married to for more than forty-five years. They had been through a lot together during that span of time. Momma tearfully said goodbye to Daddy as she lightly kissed his forehead.

As Daddy lay there pale and lifeless, the nurses and attendants quickly began to remove the IV needles and other assorted medical apparatuses that were used for his care. They did all of this with little emotion, something that I couldn't comprehend at the time. How could they be so matter of fact while my father is lying there deceased? Do they not care about him anymore? It was lost on me that they saw death daily, and that they are not as fazed by the sight as much as a layman like me are.

As I stood reflecting on Daddy's life and death, my mind wandered to the afterlife, to Heaven, and to the promise of eternal life in Christ that I believed in (and still do) as a Christian. I felt inner peace knowing that Daddy was in paradise.

I was so happy that Daddy would be united in heaven with his brother William, his sister Marion, and the child he and Momma had lost due to miscarriage. I pondered his being reunited with his father and my grandfather, Fred, and with my Great-Granddaddy and Great-Grandmother Hulsey, a thought that I would later call into question and that would challenge my own faith in true eternal forgiveness and wholeness.

I contemplated what was I to do as a twenty-five-year-old

man without a father to guide and direct me, and all I would miss learning from him as I grew into manhood. As Momma, Phil and I left the hospital headed back to Rockmart, snow began to fall our entire way home.

****

Friday, the 13th of March, 1987 was the day of Daddy's funeral. It was an overcast, blustery day with gusting winds and a spattering of rain. Reverend David Taylor of the Rockmart First Baptist Church presided over the memorial. In his eulogy, Reverend Taylor quoted a line from the book and movie *Brian's Song"* to capture what he, and all of us, believed summed up Daddy's life here on Earth:

"Fred Hulsey was a good man that loved his family, his community and all whom he came in contact with. He will be remembered fondly by so many people. And when we remember Fred, it's not how he died that we will remember but, how he lived. How he did live!"

Truer words could not have been spoken. They gave me comfort as I sat in the church pew next to Momma, gazing at all of the beautiful flowers that adorned Daddy's casket. Daddy had lived sixty-two years, and he had given so much of his life in service to the community of Rockmart. He had lived a good life, and when his family and friends recalled old memories, they spoke fondly and respectfully of him.

Momma and I worked hard to put aside the animosity we had felt toward Daddy's drinking and the actions that followed. We wanted to only remember the good times – the happier times. Daddy left the world with a good name, an accomplishment that I would later learn was a difficult struggle for him to achieve.

After Daddy's death, I continued to live at the family home on Ivy Street in Rockmart with Momma. Phil was married and owned his own home. I had purchased a house on nearby Howard Street but hadn't moved into it yet. Momma would need me to help take care of her, I thought. She would be lonely without Daddy, and I would need to be her protector and advisor in the days to come. In retrospect, I craved Momma' company. Nevertheless, I made it my personal mission to see to it that she would be loved and cared for after the loss of her husband of nearly forty-five years.

The conversations that we would have after Daddy's death were deep and sometimes painful for Momma, and difficult for me to hear. Just like any other man, Daddy wasn't perfect, and having lived with him for forty-five years had not always been a bed of roses for Momma. She would recall good times that she and Daddy had shared together since they were young teenagers.

Momma would also recall times when Daddy's temper would flare, and when he would lash out at her for what she perceived as the least little thing. I discovered through those conversations that, although he never talked about it, Daddy's childhood was not a very happy time for him.

He had been moved around from place to place after

Granddaddy's untimely death from a heart attack at the early age of thirty-one. He would live with his mother, Maw Maw Vert, and with his sister, Hope, without a man in the house to provide for them and to protect them. He was moved to his grandmother's boarding house in Rockmart from time to time where she would take care of him.

Daddy participated in many activities as a child, including the Boy Scouts, and in various sports, all of which he excelled in. But none of that could take the place of losing his father at the tender ripe age of eight years old, something that I couldn't fathom as I mourned the loss of Daddy at the age of twenty-five. Momma understood his sometimes acrimonious demeanor, given all that he had dealt with as a child. But it would provide lasting unpleasant memories for her. I would find out in the months to come that there was much more that led to his behavior.

CHAPTER SEVEN:
THE BOARD GAME

Aunt Dossie and Uncle Willie were stalwart in their support and care for Momma and Daddy during Daddy's illness. After Daddy's death, they took it upon themselves to continue looking after Momma. Many times, when they would go out for supper or on a shopping expedition, they would take Momma with them. Uncle Willie made sure that Momma's car was in proper working condition, that the oil was changed regularly, and that the tires were inflated at the correct pressure.

Momma appreciated their loving care and concern for her well-being. She and Uncle Willie enjoyed needling one another. They were like siblings, always trying to one up the other. When you put Momma and Uncle Willie together, you knew that duo would accidently and without fail create mayhem all their own.

One of Momma's and Uncle Willie's most significant high jinks involved their "partnership" in a board game being facilitated by the Ingles Supermarket chains across all of their stores. The gist of the game was that every shopper in the store could obtain a game board. Whenever you went into the store and made a purchase, you would receive a game piece. If that game piece matched one of the blank spaces on the game board, you would attach the piece to the board.

The ultimate goal of the game was to completely fill your board. Throughout the entire network of Ingles Super-markets, there would be one lucky winner, and that person would receive the grand prize of one-million dollars.

Momma and Uncle Willie devised their plan to win the loot. Utilizing only one game board, they would share the game pieces each one of them received when they shopped at Ingles. If they were the "lucky ones" who filled their board, they would claim their grand prize and split their new-found prosperity 50/50.

For weeks, Momma and Uncle Willie collected their game pieces. Each time one of them would garner a piece they didn't already have, they would get together and place it on their board. They knew that their partnership would reap great fortune for them in the end. They were successful in getting every space on their board filled, except for one. The middle piece of the board, the one that would bring them fame and fortune, continuously eluded them as they continued their pursuit of the riches. Weeks turned into a couple of months, and no one had yet claimed the grand prize from the Ingles Supermarkets.

Momma and Uncle Willie would continue their pursuit of the last piece, even as they grew weary of their prospects of winning. During the short span of the contest, Momma must have purchased more groceries than she would have when Daddy, Phil and I were with her at home. She amassed a stockpile of canned goods that I knew she could never eat by herself. She felt she had to make the purchases to have any chance of getting that last piece and claiming the spoils for Uncle Willie and herself.

One day, as the contest wore on, Uncle Willie decided to get an old jacket out of his closet to wear that he hadn't worn for some time. As he was headed outdoors that day, he slipped on the jacket. Warming his hands inside of the pockets, he felt a small piece of paper lodged into the seam of one of the pockets.

When Uncle Willie pulled the piece of paper out, excitement overtook him as he gazed at what he had in his hands. It was as if he had found a pot of gold or the Hope Diamond. There in the palms of his gigantic hands was the missing piece. All along, he had the middle piece of the board in his jacket pocket. Uncle Willie knew that he needed to act at once. There was no time to gloat about his impending affluence. That could wait until he and Momma could get to the Rockmart Ingles and stake their claim on the million bucks.

Uncle Willie phoned Momma to tell her of the thrilling news. They were going to be millionaires! Of course, after they split the bounty down the middle, they each would be receiving $500,000, minus taxes that would be owed. As usual, Uncle Sam and the Georgia Department of Revenue had to get their portion. Collectively, Momma and Uncle Willie would be netting close to $350,000 each simply by playing the Ingles' game. Not bad for a girl born in Paulding County and a boy from just outside Rockmart in Aragon, Georgia, both with only high school educations.

Uncle Willie instructed Momma to be waiting outside of her house on Ivy Street next to the road. He was going to pick her up and they would go to Ingles and claim their riches. They couldn't hide their elation from one another as they took the mile-and-a-half trek from Momma's house to the supermarket.

Arriving at the Ingles, Uncle Willie placed the winning game board under his jacket, holding it close to his six-foot, six-inch exterior for safekeeping. Momma walked with all of the confidence she could muster as they strolled through the automatic door into the supermarket. At the front of the Rockmart Ingles was a semi-elevated office area where the store manager and head cashier performed their administrative duties.

On that particular day, the female store manager was working in the front office when Momma and Uncle Willie approached to claim their grand prize. Being the curious sort of person that is customary with being a "Rock-martian," Uncle Willie didn't want everyone in the store to know that he and Momma were about to claim the one-million dollar winnings.

As he approached the office, Uncle Willie gazed suspiciously all around him to see who might be listening in to what he was about to proclaim. Seeing many shoppers and store employees nearby him, he looked up into the office directly at the manager and quietly exclaimed, "Psssst...pssst. Hey you, Store Manager. Meet us over in the 'bananers' (that is how Uncle Willie and many of us Southerners pronounce the word bananas and other words ending with the vowel "a"). We've got something to show you."

The manager was a little taken aback by the dysphoria and whispering tone of Uncle Willie's command. Nevertheless, she exited the office area and followed Uncle Willie and Momma to the produce section and to the "bananers," located very near the office, but away from the hustle and bustle of the front area. As they reached the produce aisle, Uncle Willie and Momma looked around the store with suspicion and anxiety once again, as if they were James Bond 007 looking for a wayward criminal to surprise them.

Uncle Willie held tightly to the winning game board underneath his jacket as if he was holding on to a gun, just in case the criminal was to attack. Once the coast was clear, he carefully unfurled the game board on top of a stack of the "bananers". Momma and Uncle Willie looked on silently and with great anticipation as the store manager took a close look at the game board. She could see that the board was indeed complete with all of the pieces.

As she gazed more scrupulously at the purported winning game board, the manager began shaking her head from side to side. Staring back and forth with anguish and remorse into Uncle Willie's and Momma's eyes, she sadly proclaimed that the middle piece of the board, the one that Uncle Willie had miraculously found in his jacket pocket only a couple of hours earlier, was from the previous year's game, not this year's.

Uncle Willie and Momma looked at each other with disbelief as they processed the news in their minds. Uncle Willie quickly snapped up the game board from atop the bananers, thanked the manager for her time, and embarrassingly appealed to her not to share the story of their demise with anyone. Summoning Momma, who was dumbstruck, to come with him, they hurriedly exited the store and got into Uncle Willie's vehicle.

Momma said that she and Uncle Willie didn't utter a single word on that short drive back to her home on Ivy Street, nor did they when she exited his vehicle. At that time, it was no laughing matter, but days later, Momma, Uncle Willie and the rest of our family would get a good chuckle from the outcome of their antics. To me, it always seemed that these types of things could only happen in a small town like Rockmart.

****

The spring of 1987 transitioned to the sweltering summer that is typical to us native Georgians. The intense heat and humidity could, at times, be sultry and smothering. As I sat under the shady pecan tree at our home on Ivy Street, I could look to the backyard and the place Phil and I called "the garden", and fondly recall Daddy toiling under the brutal sunlight as he tended to the vegetables that he grew for our enjoyment.

The time he spent in the garden was his "alone time", and he would not shy away from 100-degree temperatures to till the soil, plant and harvest some of the best tomatoes, cucumbers, squash, banana and cow horn peppers, okra and other tasty delights that adorned our supper table nearly each and every night. Daddy's skin would tan to a dark brown hue as he brought in the harvest of his labor. I always looked forward to the summertime for three reasons – summer break from school, baseball, and Daddy's fresh, homegrown vegetables.

Back then, Rockmart had two nine-hole golf courses. Both of them were owned by a family friend of ours, Frank Herring. Momma and Frank's wife, Ruth, were good friends and played bridge together. "Rooster," as Momma affectionately called Ruth, was one of my favorite "Rockmartians," someone whom I loved dearly, who had a wonderful sense of humor, and who had a tell-it-like-it-is approach to life. She was also an excellent cook, and I thoroughly enjoyed many dishes she offered to our family over the years, particularly when Daddy was ill with his cancer.

One hot summer day in 1987, Ruth was at our house helping Momma with freezing and canning vegetables that she had grown, harvested and given to us. This would be the first summer in many years that a crop didn't come from Daddy's garden, since he had died only a few months before. Ruth knew that, and she wanted to do something special for her dear friend. That's the way Momma and her friends operated – they helped one another in good times and bad. It was a time to be helpful, to socialize, to laugh and to cry.

Only a few days before, a fully cooked Honey Baked ham had been delivered to our house by courier as a gift from

Momma's boss and the physician who delivered both Phil and me, Dr. Charlie Smith. The ham was kept chilled by dry ice, a cooling agent that is nothing more than frozen carbon dioxide. Whenever you place the substance in water, it creates a smoky cloud that is reminiscent of the steam coming from a witch's brew or the thick fog that is pumped onto concert stages to create special effects.

Once the ham was unpacked, I secured the dry ice in our freezer for future endeavors. For me, having the dry ice in my possession was trouble waiting to happen. I cooked up all sorts of schemes to use the chunks of the frostbitten matter to please my insatiable desire to make a little mischief and have a lot of fun.

Our home on Ivy Street in Rockmart had ten total rooms—three bedrooms, a foyer (or hall, as we dubbed it), a living room, den, breakfast room, kitchen, utility room (we called this the "back porch," even though it was heated space inside the house), and one very small bathroom with a shower/tub, sink and a tiny toilet (or commode, as we called it). The bathroom was centered within the house and had two doors, one that connected to Momma's bedroom and the other to the "back porch".

I overheard Ruth exclaim to Momma that she was, "About to pee all over myself, and I need to use your bathroom!" Once I heard this, I quickly sprang into action. I ran to the freezer that was located on the "back porch" and grabbed a sizeable chunk of the dry ice.

Tacitly and expeditiously, I tiptoed my way into the bathroom, released a lump of my frozen magic potion into the commode, and then closed the lid. I hurriedly departed the bathroom, hid in my bedroom, and with great anticipation awaited the ensuing madness that was about to unfold.

Entering the bathroom, closing the doors and then lifting the lid on the smoldering cauldron (the commode), Ruth let out a thundering howl and began shouting expletives that, if I had voiced them, would have gotten my mouth washed out with soap.

Momma ran into the bathroom to assist Ruth with whatever was going on. I, in turn, enjoyed the entire proceeding and laughed hysterically in my bedroom; that is, until Momma came looking for me when she had realized what I had done to poor Ruth. I will always wonder if Ruth got to "take care of nature" in the bathroom or if she "did it" all over herself.

Momma didn't appreciate the comical nature of my prank, exclaiming, "Brad Hulsey, you are twenty-five years old, and I swear you still act like a conniving little boy! I was going to slice you some of the ham for your supper, but I think you'll need to fend for your own meal tonight after having embarrassed me. Poor Ruth, she may never come back over here again!"

I was unhappy about the ramifications of my tomfoolery, but I will always rate this as one of my top schemes of all time. Years later, whenever we would come into contact, Ruth would fondly remind me of that caper. We would always crow (after all, she was known as "Rooster") and guffaw at what had taken place.

CHAPTER EIGHT:
MYSTERY ON THE GOLF COURSE

One of the golf courses owned by Frank Herring was the Goodyear Golf Course where, in years past, Phil and I, along with many other kids of Goodyear employees, would enjoy the Christmas party and viewing of the balloons that would be flown during the Macy's Thanksgiving Day Parade in New York City. The other was Prospect Valley Golf Course, located just outside the city limits on Prospect Road.

Daddy always played the Goodyear course, having participated for several years there in a league comprised of Goodyear employees. I, therefore, preferred the Goodyear course, as well. Daddy never invited me to play with him, something I've always regretted. It would have been fun to have played golf with my father like many other young men get to do.

Only five months after Daddy's death, on a very hot and steamy August 1987 day, I decided for some strange reason to walk and play nine holes at the Goodyear course. This meant I would carry my bag and clubs over the one-and-a-half-mile terrain in the sweaty, muggy conditions, instead of driving a golf cart. I suppose I was young, cheap and nearly broke, even though I had my bi-weekly paycheck from my sales position at J.L. Lester & Son, plus my monthly City Council salary of $50.00, compliments of the taxpaying citizens of Rockmart. After an exhausting two hours of chasing my golf ball from one side of the course to another, I had worked up gallons of perspiration and the need for a drink to quench my thirst as I finished my round.

Inside the clubhouse, the snack area offered one of my favorite soft drinks, Upper 10, that was a rare find in most places. Typically, I would replenish the salt I lost while sweating it out on the course with a bag of Lance Gold-N-Cheese crackers. They were so delicious, with a salty, cheesy flavor that had just a smidgen of paprika and that gave off a spicy sensation when they met my taste buds.

The drink and snacks totaled up to sixty cents, a monetary figure that, at the time, had no real meaning to me, except that I would always make sure to have enough money on hand to satisfy my urge for the goodies. I laid down two quarters and two nickels, purchased one of the ice cold, refreshing liquid thirst quenchers and a bag of the scrumptious crackers, devoured them both in less than two minutes, and returned outside to retrieve my clubs and head on my merry way home.

When I looked off in the distance to the 9th hole fairway, I saw an amazing sight, one that caught my attention and led me back near the final green. I stared with wonder as I watched a man, having an obvious handicap with one of his legs, swing the club as he let go with one arm, hitting the ball square in the middle, pure and clean. He had slight difficulty getting in and out of the golf cart, which was being driven by a lady, his wife, I presumed. Having never been one to shy away from speaking to someone, I approached the man as he putted out and completed his round.

As he placed his putter back into his golf bag that was tightly secured to the back of the cart, I proceeded toward him with little timidity. I wanted to introduce myself and learn more about him. I greeted him with, "Good afternoon. I certainly don't mean anything by this but, I must say, you are better at golfing one-handed than I am with two."

I felt like such a fool by those words. I had just told this man that he has a handicap; not something that makes a great first impression. He looked at me over his rounded glasses with a gentle smile and said, "Why, thank you young man. I'm not much of a golfer, but I sure do enjoy hacking at the ball." The gentleman then extended his right hand toward mine in a friendly gesture and exclaimed, "My name is Lavay McCullough."

As I was offering my right hand in a handshake I said to my newly discovered acquaintance, "It's a pleasure to meet you, sir. My name is Brad Hulsey." Before I could grab hold of his large, bear-like hand, Mr. McCullough pulled his hand back toward his body and replied with a curious look on his face, "Brad Hulsey? Brad Hulsey, huh? So, Brad, who was your father?" I raised my right eyebrow with a puzzled look. How could this man have known to ask who "was" my father? Did he know that Daddy had died only five months ago, and if he did, why, and how did he know about it?

I anxiously replied, "My father was Fred Hulsey. Did you

know him, sir?" Mr. McCullough inquired, "Fred Hulsey Jr.?" I came back, "Yes sir, that was my daddy. Did you know him?" Lavay McCullough then extended his right hand out once again, taking mine into his in a warm handshake and exclaimed, "Yes, Brad. I knew Fred. Fred was a good man, and I'm sorry to hear of his passing. It's a pleasure to meet you." After Mr. McCullough had introduced me to his lovely wife, Gladys, I continued with my interrogation, "How did you know Daddy? Did you and he grow up together?"

With an uncomfortable and hurried demeanor about him Mr. McCullough abruptly offered these parting words, "I knew Fred most of my life, Brad. I grew up here in Rockmart and in other places. I haven't lived in Rockmart for several years, but I've always kept in touch with what's going on here. As I stated, it was a pleasure meeting you, but my wife and I need to be going now."

Then with another quick, firm handshake and final well wishes and goodbyes, Lavay McCullough loaded his clubs into his vehicle and drove away with his wife, leaving me with a wonderstruck mind and an abundance of unanswered questions.

I sensed a hint of apprehension from Mr. McCullough as he and his wife departed, almost as if he was wanting to say more to me but couldn't, or wouldn't, or shouldn't. I wanted to know and I needed to know more about this unassuming, reserved man I had just met. I thought, surely, Momma would know more about him and the mystery that surrounded our confrontation. I quickly loaded my clubs into the trunk of my Pontiac 6000 STE and rushed home to tell Momma about my recent encounter.

As I walked into our family's lovely brick home there on Ivy Street, I felt a certain uneasiness from my short discussion with Lavay McCullough, and a longing for the presence of Daddy to clarify what was and wasn't said. But he wasn't going to be there, except perhaps in spirit. I would need to tell Momma about my meeting and get the answers to the questions I so desperately wanted and needed.

As was customary on a summer's evening, Momma was in the kitchen preparing supper, fraught with many of the delicious vegetables that she and Ruth Herring had canned and frozen. The aroma inside the house was divine. I asked Momma to turn off the stove for a little while. I needed to tell her about my unusual meeting at the golf course and all that had transpired. We moved into the den, where we could sit comfortably and talk.

Excitedly, I told Momma about meeting Lavay McCullough and what a nice man he was. I continued to chatter about how Mr. McCullough was such a good golfer in spite of his apparent handicap, and of how he had known Daddy and had offered his sympathy about his death. Without hesitation, Momma stopped my conversation with an aroused look on her face and inquired, "What did Lavay say about your father?"

I was surprised from Momma's tone and nervous behavior, and by the fact that she purposefully called the gentleman by his first name. I informed her of how Mr. McCullough spoke kindly of Daddy, of how he was a good man, and how he had grown up in and around Rockmart. Momma replied, "Yes, he would say that. Lavay McCullough is a fine Christian man, a Baptist pastor, I believe. As I recall, he was stricken with polio as a young child. How nice of him to say such good things about your father."

As I had sensed throughout my conversation with Lavay McCullough and his ultimate rapid departure, I also perceived some trepidation in Momma as she awaited my next question. I suspected there was so much more to the relationship between Daddy and Lavay McCullough, much more that Momma, Mr. McCullough or even Daddy was or had been willing to disclose. I would soon learn that my suspicions were correct, to a degree that I could have never have fathomed.

I quizzed Momma on how she knew of Lavay McCullough, and how she knew that he was a pastor and had been stricken with polio as a child. Frustratingly, I exclaimed, "Okay, Momma. I don't know what's going on here. First, I meet Lavay McCullough and, yes, while he was very kind, he seemed somewhat evasive in his answers to my inquisition. And now, here you are, acting the very same way. You know I don't like secrets or surprises, so for the life of me, will you please let me know what this is all about?"

Momma hesitated for a moment and took a long, deep breath, appearing to be gathering her thoughts. She let out a long sigh, looked at me with her tender, loving blue eyes and said, "Stay seated, Son. I'm going to put supper away. We can eat later, if we feel like it. This could take a while. I have a story I need to tell you."

As Momma went into the kitchen, I sat in the den with wonder and anticipation as I awaited her return. What was she about to tell me? What was I going to learn from the story she was going to tell me? Why was there so much mystery and suspense surrounding my meeting with Lavay McCullough? The pots and pans clanged as Momma began clearing supper from the stove and placing it in the refrigerator for safekeeping. As she readied to return to our discussion, I could hear her muttering under her breath, "Help me, Lord. Oh Lordy mercy, help me please."

CHAPTER NINE:
TRUTH

I readied myself for whatever lie ahead, but I just wasn't sure what was about to come. As Momma reluctantly walked back into the den and sat down in her easy chair, she gazed at me, leaned forward, and asked me to forgive her for never having told me about what she was preparing to disclose to me.

Momma said that Daddy would not have wanted me or Phil to know the story she was about to relay, but that she felt compelled by my excessive curiosity and from my brief encounter with Lavay McCullough to tell me all that she knew. For all of my life, no one, not a soul, had uttered a word or even gave a hint of what I was about to learn.

I would have preferred to have heard it from Daddy. After all, he was supposed to be my protector, the one whom I trusted most, most admired and most loved – right up there with Momma. He had kept this secret that was about to be revealed to me for twenty-five years. Once the secret was disclosed, it would build a great chasm between my now deceased father and me—his youngest son, which would last for over two-and-a-half decades. As Momma began to share the story, I was taken back to a Rockmart I never knew at a time I never knew. The year was 1930...

Beginning in late 1929 and lasting until the late 1930s, the Great Depression brought devastating effects to the United States and, in fact, the entire world, creating terrible living and working conditions in countries rich and poor. Its' origin was in the United States, after the fall in stock prices that began around September 4, 1929.

The Great Depression became a worldwide phenomenon with the stock market crash of October 29, 1929, commonly referred to as "Black Tuesday". Personal income, tax revenue, profits and prices dropped, while international trade plunged by more than 50%. Unemployment in the U.S. rose to 25% and in some countries as high as 33%.

Cities during the Great Depression were hit hard, especially those dependent on heavy industry. Construction was virtually halted in many countries.

Farming and rural areas suffered as crop prices fell by approximately 60%. Facing plummeting demand with few alternate sources of jobs, areas dependent on primary sector industries such as mining and logging suffered the most.

While the Great Depression did have an impact on the Rockmart citizens and businesses, they fared better than many other areas. The Goodyear Mill officially opened on December 12, 1929, providing over three-hundred jobs and income for many of the town's residents, with a starting total payroll of $500,000. During that time, the mill's primary focus was to supply rubberized fabric to the Gadsden, Alabama tire plant.

Years later, during the World War II era, fulfilling U.S. Department of Defense contracts would be the mill's mission. With the advent of the single largest boost in the economy of Rockmart's history, the city-owned electric power plant was sold so that the city could finance the new roads, water works, water lines, sewers, sidewalks and other vital infrastructure needed to build a small city within a city.

Being a community partner and a good corporate citizen was important to Goodyear and crucial to its success. Goodyear purchased three-hundred eighteen acres of land in Rockmart and began developing the property earlier in 1929. Over a large parcel of the property, directly across from the mill, the company constructed the Goodyear Village that offered homes to their employees and townspeople at a reduced cost.

Goodyear donated a smaller parcel of raw, undeveloped land for their employees to grow their own vegetables and raise livestock on, providing them an opportunity to grow and harvest food for their families. Years later, Goodyear would go on to construct a tennis court, a day school for the children of employees and the Goodyear Golf Course.

Another employer that offered job opportunities to the residents of Rockmart in 1930 was the Southern States Portland Cement Company. Like Goodyear, Southern States afforded competitive wages to its employees. Slate mines in Rockmart and the nearby community of Van Wert, originally founded and operated by Welsh settlers, would come and go from the late nineteenth century on into the 20th and 21st century.

Many of the homes and landmarks in Rockmart were constructed of the slate found from these quarries. The Monarch Brick Company, which produced brick with the raised insignia "ROCKMART" cast upon it became a victim of the economic woes surrounding the Great Depression, closing its doors after twenty-nine years of existence in 1929.

In addition to the property Goodyear offered to the tenants and residents, many locals in the Rockmart area had farms of their own. Agriculture was big business in Rockmart and the surrounding communities, where raising livestock, milking cows, poultry and eggs, vegetables and other forms of vital foods was commonplace among many of the residents of Rockmart.

My great-grandfather, William "Bill" Hulsey, and my great-grandmother, Corrie Hulsey, owned and operated their own farm in the neighboring community of Van Wert. There, they raised their own food and grew a little cotton. My great-grandfather was out of work at the start of the Great Depression, thanks to a few personal "misjudge-ments" on his own behalf and a tendency to indulge in certain rogue activities.

The same lot in life held true for my grandfather, Fred A. Hulsey, Sr. in 1930. He worked as a meat cutter at Heaton's Meat Market in Rockmart, owned by relatives of my grandmother, Verdie Mae Hulsey or, as we called her, Maw Maw Vert. Granddaddy Hulsey had also worked as a meat cutter at J.O. Gurley's Grocery and Meats, located at what is known as the "Goodyear corner" at Goodyear

60 CENTS

Avenue and Piedmont Avenue in Rockmart. Gurley's proudly advertised on their storefront and three delivery trucks, "Fancy Groceries and Western Meats".

What the grocer did not tout was the fact that many of the townsfolk didn't just shop there for their food essentials. J.O. Gurley's was a gathering place for locals after the Goodyear Mill would let out, along with the Trolley Car Café located next door. There, many people would meet to set up gambling and other sporting events.

My Hulsey grandfathers were no exception and were heavily involved in the gaming that took place there at Gurley's and, particularly, the Trolley Car Café. Eventually, Granddaddy Hulsey would lose his job at Gurley's due to his excessive and obsessive gambling activities, and his tendency to overindulge in the partaking of alcoholic beverages.

It was "like father, like son," because Great-Granddaddy Hulsey enjoyed his adult beverages, as well, along with being heavily involved in games of chance, even though he had little or no finances to spare. Both grandfathers would have various run-ins with local law authorities as they did their carousing around Rockmart and Van Wert. Together, as a father and son team, they were usually up to no good.

Although the mischievous sort no matter the circumstances, Granddaddy Hulsey was lesser of a wrongdoer when he was not under the influence of Great-Granddaddy Hulsey; and, of the distilled spirits. But he did love to gamble. In June of 1930, Daddy was just six-years old, and his sister Hope was less than a year old. Maw Maw Vert's 24th birthday was coming soon on August 8th. Little did they know that their lives soon would be thrown into a tailspin, as would those of so many others.

Details were sketchy at best coming from Momma, simply because she and Daddy hadn't spoken much about the matter, nor had anyone else, for that matter. Daddy did utter a few inconsequential remarks from time to time about all that had transpired, but never within an earshot of Phil or me. Over the years, Momma would learn more from stories shared by her immediate family, friends, co-workers and persons anxious to tell a story that had absolutely nothing to do with them, but who liked to appear to "be in the know".

The covert story Momma would finally reveal to me began unfolding on June 19, 1930. On that day, being unem-ployed and with little to attend to, both Granddaddy and Great-Granddaddy Hulsey decided to rustle up a game of poker at the Hulsey farm, just a few miles outside of Rockmart, in Van Wert. There, three men, two who worked at the Goodyear Mill and one at the New Way Dry Cleaning Plant, arrived via taxicab after work to participate in the gaming activities.

My grandfathers had been drinking excessively all day long, and were willing to place all of their money on the table in a game of chance poker. The consumption of alcohol continued as the men joined my grandfathers, imbibing on beer and homebrew as they continued to deal the cards. One of the three men visiting the farm decided that he wanted no part of the game, and declared that he was heading back toward town. Others were present but not participating in the game, as Momma recalled.

One of those present was a local taxi driver who had driven the three men from nearby Gurley's Grocery to the farm. The other two were Great-Granddaddy's other son (and Granddaddy's brother), Ray Hulsey, and Tom Hicks, who was married to Myrtle, one of Great-Granddaddy's daughters (and Granddaddy's and Ray's sister). Momma supposed that these three men were so amused with the game that they didn't need to be a part, or they didn't have any money to gamble away.

As Granddaddy, Great-Granddaddy Hulsey and the two other men participating in the poker game continued to drink heavily and ventured further into their game of chance, my grandfathers began to lose their shirts, so to speak. Most, if not all of their money was fleeting away. They became angry and frustrated as they sought to recoup their losses.

Without any regard for the two men, their lives, and their families (both the visitors and their own), Momma said that my grandfathers began brandishing hand guns, or at least one of them did. They walked behind the two men who had taken most of their monetary loot and suddenly...BANG! They shot one of the men in the back of his head. A few seconds later...another BANG! They had shot the other man in the back of his head.

The two men laid there in a bloody pool, both of them shot

dead; murdered in two senseless, cold-blooded killings by my grandfathers. The third man, who had left and walked back into town, returned to the farm, viewed the grisly scene and then, in a flash...BANG! He was shamelessly shot to death by my grandfathers, as well.

When I heard all of this, my face became flushed as I was overcome by a range of thoughts and emotions. I was scared of what I was hearing. I felt guilt and remorse for what my grandfathers had done to these three men, as well as to their loved ones left behind. I was filled with anger toward my grandfathers for their actions. Most of all, I felt sick to my stomach over having not known this gruesome story and in not having heard it from Daddy. Why hadn't he told me about this, I wondered? Momma told me, "There's more to the story, Son."

"The three men who were murdered were all young men with families, just like your Granddaddy Hulsey. One of them was named Cliff Jones, another was a Harper man (I would learn later that Mr. Harper went by the name of Lige), and the third man...Momma hesitated and gasped for breath. Son, the third man was named Ernest McCullough. He was Lavay McCullough's father."

My mouth opened aghast, and I began to tremble at this news. Only a few hours earlier I had stood in front of a kind and decent man whom my grandfathers had senselessly and in an act of cold-blooded murder taken the life of his father. I hung my head and began to weep as Momma comforted me. I wondered aloud how Lavay McCullough could have spoken to me without any anger or hatred evident in his heart.

How could it be that I never knew that all of this had taken place some fifty-seven years ago? Why hadn't Daddy told me all of this, instead of my having some chance experience of meeting a kind man that I didn't know and to ultimately find out that my grandfathers had maliciously murdered his father?

Did Lavay McCullough ever get to know his father, to know what he was like, what he valued, what he desired out of his life and for his family? How could Lavay McCullough have said such nice words about Daddy, knowing that Daddy's father and grandfather had taken his father's life?

For me, there were so many unanswered questions, and so much sorrow, guilt and confusion in my heart and mind. I wanted to apologize to Lavay McCullough for what my family had wrought on him and his family. After several minutes, I wiped my eyes and timidly asked Momma to continue the story.

Momma recounted the aftermath of the murders to the best of her recollection...My grandfathers were purported to have loaded the bodies of their three murder victims onto a wooden wagon they "borrowed" (stole) from my Great-Granddaddy's neighbor. Blood flowed everywhere as Great-Granddaddy and Granddaddy hurriedly threw the lifeless corpses into the bed of the wagon.

Great-Granddaddy Hulsey hitched up his old grey mule to

the wagon, and he and Granddaddy began a journey up an abandoned road near Springdale Road and the Atlanta Highway with their casualties in tow. They decided that they could hide the dead bodies in an old abandoned well they were familiar with. The old well was located next to a seldom-used unpaved road near the railroad tracks.

They were severely inebriated, and their devious plan was to hide the bodies, and hope that no one would know of or suspect that anything had taken place. Once they reached their destination, Momma stated that my grandfathers heaved the bodies of the three murdered men face-down into the abandoned well.

Having the bloodied and mangled lifeless carcasses secured in the well and, in their estimation, out of sight from anyone, they returned to the farm to consider what they had done. There, they weighed the implications of their actions and how they could maintain the "cover up" of what they had wrought.

Furthering the story, Momma recalled that on the day after the murders, a man and his son were hiking in the area near the well, looking for bee trees for honey. As they happened upon the abandoned well, they looked down inside the dark hole and gazed upon a man's blood-stained foot sticking straight up into the air. As they looked more closely, they could see that there were more bodies entombed in the well.

The man and son hurried back into town to alert the authorities about their gruesome finding. Once the police arrived at the scene, they found a pack of bloodied playing cards wrapped in a piece of bloodstained paper, the hair of a grey mule, the marred tracks of a wagon, as well as a trail of blood leading up to the well where the three murder victim's bodies had been carelessly dumped. After preparing the evidence they had found and removing the three deceased men from the well, the police took the bodies in to town.

Everyone in Rockmart and Van Wert knew that William Hulsey was the only man in town with a grey mule, so the local and county police paid my Great-Granddaddy a visit at his farm in Van Wert. Upon searching the farm, the authorities discovered the ramshackle remains of an old wagon in Great-Granddaddy's barn, with the bed of the wagon missing.

There were five men arrested and incarcerated in the Rockmart City Jail for suspicion of the murders: Great-Granddaddy Hulsey, Granddaddy Hulsey, my great-uncle Ray Hulsey, my great-uncle Tom Hicks, and L.E. McCullough, the taxi driver who had driven the three murder victims to Great-Granddaddy's farm. The local authorities, the Solicitor General, and the Court System moved quickly to bind over, arraign and schedule a trial date for the five men.

Eventually, the authorities would determine that, in their findings and professional opinions, the evidence didn't point toward Ray Hulsey, Tom Hicks or L.E. McCullough as having any role in the murders of Cliff Jones, Lige

Harper or Ernest McCullough. They would only be charged as accessories to the crimes.

On the other hand, Granddaddy and Great-Granddaddy Hulsey would be the only two who would be formally charged and eventually arraigned for the murders of the three men. My grandfathers were ordered to be taken to Rome, Georgia and held without bond until the Grand Jury convened and determined whether or not there was enough evidence that would warrant an indictment in either of the three murders.

I had to ask Momma to stop for a while. All of this coming at me at once was overwhelming. The details she was sharing coupled with the fact that I was hearing it for the first time ever had my head pounding and my heart racing with anxiety. My brain was dizzied with an overabundance of curiosity and bewilderment. It was inconceivable for me at this point to comprehend how all of this could have taken place and how I had never heard a single word about it all up until now. Why had it been hidden from me and Phil for our entire lives? What will Phil think about all of it?

Momma asked if I wanted her to warm up the supper she had prepared right before she took me along this storied journey into my family's history. I knew I needed to eat, but at this juncture there was no way I could even think of eating. At this point, all I wanted was for Momma to continue the story. I told Momma that I would take something to drink but in no way could I ingest any food right then. She poured us a glass of iced sweet tea with lemon, and taking a seat she forged ahead with the drama...

According to Momma, Daddy had opined on several occasions that there was "a rush to judgment" by the judicial system due to the interest and outrage within the community. She said that the majority of the Rockmart and Polk County residents wanted quick justice to be handed down over the senseless and barbaric slayings of the three men.

In an unprecedented move, the February 1930 Polk County Grand Jury, that had already been recessed, was hurriedly called back into special session by Polk County Superior Court Judge Price Edwards to hear the charges against my grandfathers. This jury convened in early July of 1930, only a few weeks after the murders occurred and only three weeks after my grandfathers had been arrested, to specifically deal with the charges of murder against them.

Family and friends of my grandfathers hired an attorney out of Atlanta to represent them, William G. McRae. Momma said that Mr. McRae was a stately man and served at that time in the Georgia House of Representatives, as well as being an accomplished jurist. She said that McRae asked for a continuance of the case and that the evidence be allowed to be heard during the regular August term of the Grand Jury.

In July 1930, at the special-called session of the February 1930 Grand Jury, after there appeared to be enough circumstantial evidence present to continue the process, my Granddaddy and Great-Granddaddy Hulsey were formerly arraigned in the Polk County Superior Court for the murder of Cliff Jones. Solicitor General S.W. Ragsdale (also known as Colonel Ragsdale for his service in World War I) had earlier determined, with the court's concurrence, that there would be separate trials for each of the three victims. My grandfathers each entered a plea of "Not Guilty" to the murder of Cliff Jones.

Defense attorney McRae pleaded with the court that he needed the time to mount a proper defense, and that he hadn't had enough time to talk with my grandfathers regarding the case. His request fell on deaf ears from the court. They were indicted by the Grand Jury for each murder, with the first trial date set for July 14, 1930. The first trial would only be for the murder of Cliff Jones.

The evidence presented during the trial of the State vs. William Hulsey, alias Bill Hulsey, and Fred Hulsey was mostly circumstantial. According to the *Legal Dictionary*, a subsection of the *Free Dictionary*, circumstantial evidence is: *"Information and testimony by a party in a civil or criminal action that permit conclusions that indirectly establish the existence or nonexistence of a fact or event that the party seeks to prove. Circumstantial evidence is also known as indirect evidence. It is distinguished from direct evidence, which, if believed, proves the existence of a particular fact without any inference of presumption required. Circumstantial evidence related to a series of facts other than the particular fact sought to be proved. The party offering circumstantial evidence argues that this series of facts, by reason and experience, is so closely associated with the fact to be proved that the fact to be proved may be inferred simply from the existence of the circumstantial evidence."*

For a simple man like me, I deduce that circumstantial evidence is a hypothesis of what happened without much hard evidence, and/or without an eyewitness to the crime.

Momma's recollection of the trial was that it was short in length – only a matter of two or three days. She said that many of the county residents set aside their work and daily chores to attend the trial or just to be near the Polk County Courthouse in Cedartown. On one particular evening, after he had mustered up enough energy and desire to discuss the case, Daddy shared with Momma that he felt the evidence just wasn't solid enough to return a conviction against his father and grandfather.

Daddy told Momma that the prosecution didn't have enough time to fully investigate all of the potential participants in the murders of Jones, Harper and McCullough, and that Solicitor General Ragsdale, and the presiding judge in the case, the Honorable Price Edwards, were solely out to please the curious, revenge-seeking public, and to make a name for themselves on a much higher level than just locally for political reasons.

Daddy also deduced that the defense attorney, William G. McRae, wasn't allowed the necessary time and availability to interview his father and grandfather, nor the local authorities who were bringing the case forward against his father and grandfather. Nevertheless, after the commencement of the trial, and with the majority of the evidence having been presented being circumstantial in nature, Granddaddy and Great-Granddaddy Hulsey were found guilty and convicted for the murder of Cliff Jones on July 16, 1930, only twenty-seven days after the barbaric murders had occurred.

I was shaken by all that Momma was sharing with me. I implored of her why she hadn't told me about all of this a long time ago. Why did she keep it all to herself for so many years, just like Daddy and, for that matter, the entire family and community? For her part, Momma shared that Daddy had asked her to not tell Phil or me about it all. For some reason, he never wanted us to know the truth about our grandfathers.

I stopped for another gulp of tea. I swear, I nearly drank a gallon as I listened to and processed all of the information Momma was relaying to me. It was such an overwhelming sensation of so many emotions I was experiencing. My Daddy had hidden all of this from me for over twenty-five years. He hadn't uttered one word about what his father and grandfather, my flesh and blood, had done. I began to reflect on how Daddy had told me years ago that Granddaddy had died at such a young age from a heart attack.

As my mind wandered with thoughts and questions, I gathered myself and looked back to Momma and stared into her eyes. They were very telling, as if there was much more that she hadn't shared with me. I knew the story couldn't end at the guilty verdicts. As I poured the remainder of the tea into my glass, I inquired of Momma what took place after the guilty verdicts had been rendered.

With her hands shaking, Momma nervously lit up a cigarette, blew out a large puff of smoke, let out another of countless sighs, and continued with her retrospection of the events. By now, I thought I had heard the worst of the gruesome details, and that nothing could top what had already been revealed. Little did I know.

The aftermath of the verdicts was even more surreal, according to Momma. My grandfathers were housed in the Polk County Jail as they awaited Judge Edwards' sentence. The townspeople of Rockmart, as well as people all over Georgia and the United States as a whole weren't satisfied just by the guilty verdicts. They needed more. They wanted swift justice to prevail. They desired for my grandfathers to receive the same consequence as their three victims had received at their murderous hands.

They wanted Bill and Fred Hulsey to be made responsible for the senseless murders of these three men, and they got it. Perhaps their desires had validity. After all, who of us wouldn't want such vicious murderers off the streets for good and have them ultimately pay the price for their abhorrent bloodletting.

Throughout the process my grandfathers continued to maintain their innocence, even after the guilty verdicts. They argued that there had been a rush to judgement, and that there were others responsible for the heinous killings, namely the taxi driver, L.E. McCullough, and Tom Hicks.

Since the inception of the trial, Solicitor General Ragsdale had sought the death penalty for my grandfathers. As Momma relayed this, I thought to myself that, given the fact that almost all of the evidence presented in the case was circumstantial, and that the convictions came less than four weeks after the murders and impending arrests, there was no way the judge would throw down the gauntlet and issue a death sentence to my grandfathers.

All I could think of was that, while the murders and the convictions of my grandfathers had been kept secret from me for my entire life, there was no way that a death sentence against my grandfathers, if carried out, could have been hidden from me. I guess that was foolish thinking on my part, as Momma would soon convey.

Judge Edwards' decision on the sentences for my grandfathers was swift. The sentences were, also, harsh. One day after the convictions, only four weeks to the day after the murders had taken place, Granddaddy and Great-Granddaddy Hulsey were sentenced to death by execution in Georgia's electric chair at the State Prison in Milledgeville for the murder of Cliff Jones. Both of their executions were scheduled to be carried out on the same day, sometime in late August of 1930 (Momma couldn't recall the specific date), only two months after the murders.

It was eventually determined by the court that there was no need for the County and State to hold additional trials for the murders of Ernest McCullough and Lige Harper. The guilty verdicts and ultimate death sentences had been rendered for the murder of Cliff Jones.

60 CENTS

****

The light of the day had long since turned to darkness. I was sick to my stomach, mainly because of the heart-wrenching news Momma had shared with me. She consoled me as I began to shake, perhaps from the enormity of what I had learned, along with the fact that I hadn't eaten in several hours.

Momma asked me if I wanted her to heat up the now-chilled supper she had left on the stove. I began to cry out, "Why? Why? Why did all of this take place. How? How? How could Daddy have hidden this from me for all of these years – all of the way up to his death?"

I silently mused that the same blood that flowed through the veins of my grandfathers was flowing through my veins. The blood became a rush of tears as I sobbed uncontrollably. Once again, I was saddened by the murders, particularly that of Lavay McCullough's father, Ernest McCullough. My heart was aching for each of the victim's families, for Maw Maw Vert and Aunt Hope. They all experienced a huge void that would carry on with them for the remainder of their lives by the loss of their loved ones.

My sentiments toward Daddy, however, were mixed. On one hand, it was dispiriting to think of the effect all of this had on him. Daddy had lost his brother William in the terrible scalding incident when he was only two-years old. The next year, he lost his sister Marion, she having been stillborn. And now, I find out that he would soon be losing his father, his perceived caretaker and protector, as well as his grandfather, in as gruesome a manner than one could perceive – the electric chair. That is a burden above and beyond what any child should have to bear.

On the other hand, Daddy went to his grave without sharing any of this with me or Phil, his two sons – his flesh and blood. As I was saddened for Daddy, I was also enraged with bitterness toward him for keeping all of this a secret. Daddy wasn't around for me to vent my anger and frustrations with him. I suddenly felt animosity toward him that I stubbornly refused to rid myself of.

****

As the evening wore on, Momma shared the remainder of what she had learned about Granddaddy and Great-Granddaddy's fate after their death sentences had been handed down. There was no way I could have imagined how much more to the tragedy there was.

After the sentences had been handed down, my grandfathers were taken to the Floyd County Jail, where they would be incarcerated until their transfer to the State Prison in Milledgeville for their executions in late August 1930. Along with their attorney, William G. McRae, my grandfathers appealed their verdicts to the Georgia Supreme Court.

The August 1930 execution date had long since passed before the Georgia Supreme Court eventually upheld the verdict of the lower court. A new date of execution had to be scheduled. My grandfathers appeared in the Polk

County Superior Court, and the judge issued a new date of execution for July 1931.

A few days before the scheduled executions, my grandfathers were transported by sheriff's deputies from Rome to Milledgeville for their sentences to be carried out. As not only an accomplished attorney, but also as a respected State Representative from Fulton County, William G. McRae had a direct connection to Georgia's Governor (and future U.S. Senator), Richard B. Russell.

Only twenty-four hours before the executions were to have taken place in July 1931, McRae was able to convince Governor Russell to grant a sixty-day respite to my grandfathers, on the ground that Representative McRae was attending the sessions of the Legislature and required additional time to prepare for a request for clemency hearing. Momma supposed that Governor Russell was paying a political favor to McRae. She said that in true political fashion, Governor Russell cited code that suggested that any attorney who served in the Georgia Legislature would be excused in any cases that took place during the legislative session.

There would be several other appeals to the Georgia Supreme Court and stays issued by Governor Russell that would continue to prolong the executions from being carried out. It finally came down to one last attempt for clemency, and it was denied by the Georgia Supreme Court in the summer of 1932. Governor Russell refused to intervene.

Judge J.H. Hutcheson of the Polk County Superior Court set the date of execution, this time, and for the final time, for November 4, 1932. All at once, I had come to the realization that not only were Granddaddy and Great-Granddaddy convicted murderers, but they would also meet their ultimate demise in Georgia's electric chair.

Deep in thought, I asked Momma to halt the storytelling for a few moments. I needed to reflect for a while and collect my thoughts, and my composure. Once again, I pondered how all of this could have taken place in that same small town – Rockmart, and I had never heard anything about it.

I recalled how, years ago, that mean old neighbor of ours, Ms. Elizabeth Carter, had run Phil and me out of the Braswell's yard as we played, calling us "nothing but old Hulseys." Yes, we were very young at the time, but as we ran into Daddy's arms for comfort, why didn't he tell us what the real meaning of Ms. Carter's words was?

It sounds deranged, but even at that point in my life, I would have rather learned all of this directly from my own father rather than having to learn it after his death. My anger and frustration with Daddy continued. Momma's story continued, as well. The time was approaching mid-night.

Momma had remembered the exact date that the executions would take place because of another significant historical occurrence that was unfolding at that same time. Franklin Delano Roosevelt, affectionately known as FDR, was seeking the presidency for the first time. Both Momma and Daddy sang their praises of FDR and believed that he was the right man, at the right place and time, to lead toward solving all of the country's woes. In retrospect, for that time in history, they were probably right.

FDR was taking on the incumbent, President Herbert Hoover, who was an accomplished businessman, statesman and politician, but who had led the country into the Great Depression. Most people blamed Hoover for the country's demise, and many felt that Roosevelt would be the answer to solving the problems the country had been facing.

In Georgia, Governor Richard B. Russell was seeking to fill the unexpired term of the deceased U.S. Senator for the State of Georgia, William J. Harris, who hailed from Cedartown and who had died in Washington, D.C. a few months prior. Election Day was slated for Tuesday, November 8, 1932, only four days after the scheduled executions on Friday, November 4, 1932.

Since all appeals had been exhausted for my grandfathers, and given the fact that he was embroiled in a Senate campaign and, at the same time, was supporting FDR for President, Momma said that Governor Russell didn't feel the need to be present at the executions. Feeling he had the Senate seat well in hand, Russell decided that he would make a swing into North Carolina to campaign for FDR. He would, instead, give his Executive Secretary, who would remain in the state capital of Atlanta, full authority to ensure that the executions took place.

My grandfathers' executions were set to take place at 10 a.m. on November 4th. Momma recalled that both of them were worn and frazzled from all of the hoopla surrounding the whirlwind journey that eventually brought them to the State Prison in Milledgeville to meet their ultimate fate. During the morning of the executions, my grandfathers were prepared for the electrocutions by having their heads shaved, as well as one of their legs. They were held in separate holding cells. Each of them were offered a last meal, and they were each given last rites by a minister.

Soon before the designated time of execution, with the minister still within the walls of his cell, my Granddaddy Fred quickly pulled out a razor that he had somehow hidden in his pants pocket, loudly proclaimed his guilt and his father's innocence in the murders of Cliff Jones, Lige Harper and Ernest McCullough, and proceeded to slash his own throat and wrists. He evidently wanted to commit suicide rather than face the indignation of the electric chair. When I heard this, I cried out, "My God! How much more can there be to this story?"

Momma rubbed my shoulder for a moment and continued on. The prison warden had the medical examiner and several of the guards to tend to Granddaddy's wounds. He bled profusely, and the execution clothing supplied by the prison was the color of crimson as they placed my grandfather's limp body onto a gurney.

The execution was delayed for several hours while the prison personnel did their best to stop the bleeding. The medical examiner feared that Granddaddy would succumb to his wounds and that, ultimately, the execution would have to be halted. They wanted to carry out the sentence as ordered, and not allow Granddaddy the final say in his life.

As I heard Momma share that tidbit, I was totally flabbergasted. Could the medical examiner really be concerned about executing Granddaddy at that point? Evidently so. I deduced that the sentence had to be carried out in accordance with state law.

The prison warden, the medical examiner and the attendants didn't know exactly what to do. They wanted to carry out the sentence, and they needed direction from someone higher than them. In 1932, many places didn't have a telephone. Until he was able to speak with Governor Russell, his Executive Secretary ordered that the executions be delayed. It would take several anxious moments for Governor Russell's Executive Secretary to reach the Governor via telephone.

The Governor was eventually located in High Point, North Carolina, and was advised to contact his office through an Associated Press message. When he was able to speak via phone to his executive secretary, Governor Russell was told of how Granddaddy Hulsey had attempted to take his own life, and that he was in grave danger of bleeding to death.

Through his Executive Secretary, Governor Russell ordered the prison personnel to halt the executions so that they could provide adequate medical attention to Granddaddy Hulsey. Once Granddaddy was stabilized, Russell gave the order to continue with the execution process. After more than three hours of diligently applying handmade cloth bandages to Granddaddy's wounds, the warden determined that Granddaddy Hulsey was well enough to execute.

The prison personnel helped my grandfather off of the gurney that held his near lifeless body. They assisted him to the execution chamber where Georgia's electric chair, known as "Ol' Sparky," awaited its next victim. Granddaddy was clad in an undershirt, trousers, socks and shoes, all covered with his own blood.

The prison guards strapped Granddaddy Hulsey tightly into the chair and applied the electrodes to his shaved head and legs. These would send the electrical charge throughout his body. While all of this was taking place, Granddaddy was crying out, "God help me! Lord save me!" After reading from Psalm 23, the prison chaplain asked Granddaddy if he had any final words to say before his execution.

Summoning up what little strength he had in his weakened body, Granddaddy uttered, "Please tell my father that I will meet him in Heaven," alluding to the fact that soon after his execution, it would then be Great-Granddaddy Hulsey's turn to meet his maker. Momma said that Granddaddy shouted out a confession to the murders and proclaimed that he was the only one guilty and not his father. And then, after having lived for only thirty-one years, Granddaddy Hulsey had one last declaration to offer before the electrical shock would be sent through his body.

60 CENTS

"One other thing," Granddaddy exclaimed. "I wish you would take the 60 cents in my pocket and send it to my little girl."

As he was about to give his life in payment for his sins, Granddaddy wanted his daughter Hope to have all that he had left to his name. As he was being blindfolded, Granddaddy Hulsey repeatedly prayed to God to help him and to save him. At approximately 1:45 p.m., the execution was carried out.

The medical examiner said that Granddaddy died faster than any man he had ever witnessed being executed in the electric chair. It took only fifteen seconds. Had Granddaddy made peace with God after all he had done, I wondered? Or could it simply have been the extreme loss of blood he had experienced that caused the execution to take place so easily?

After removing Granddaddy's lifeless, deceased body from the electric chair, the prison guards hurriedly wiped away the blood that had flowed all over the chair and prepared it for Great-Granddaddy Hulsey's execution. Great-Granddaddy had requested that he be clad in a suit, white shirt and tie for his execution.

As he was led to the electric chair, Great-Granddaddy Hulsey proclaimed his innocence in the commission of the murders, stating that he had been present when they occurred and had participated in the attempted cover-up. Electricity was then surged through his body for nearly four minutes until he was dead, at 2 p.m. Momma said that

Daddy always fretted about how Granddaddy Hulsey had always taken the blame for his father's transgressions, and how Great-Granddaddy would willingly allow him to do so.

He had always wondered if his father had indeed acted alone in the murders or if he was making a last-ditch effort toward saving Great-Granddaddy's trip to the electric chair. Perhaps this explained why many years prior Daddy had called Great-Granddaddy Hulsey "the biggest son-of-a-bitch who ever lived".

After a brief pause to allow me to gather my thoughts, Momma then informed me that this was the first and only time that a father and son had been executed on the same day in Georgia's electric chair. All I could rouse up in my mind was, "What kind of historical record is that?" Certainly, nothing to boast about, or to share with one another at family gatherings. I did eventually share the secret revealed to me with Phil. He, like I, was taken aback and mortified at what had been kept from us. In Phil's case, it had been twenty-eight years.

Another historically significant occurrence took place only four days after my grandfathers' executions. On November 8, 1932, Franklin Delano Roosevelt was elected President of the United States, easily defeating the incumbent Republican President, Herbert Hoover. Only two months afterward, Richard B. Russell would exit the Governor's office and move on to Washington, D.C. as Georgia's junior U.S. Senator, having been elected to serve the remainder of the deceased Senator William J. Harris's term.

CHAPTER TEN:
AFTERMATH

By now, I had heard enough, and both Momma and I were exhausted from what seemed like the longest day of my life. All in a period of a few hours, I went from the small-town boy turned to man who didn't know much about his surname's history, to learning that both his grandfather and great-grandfather were convicted murderers and had died in the electric chair.

I couldn't take any more. I was tired, I was perplexed, I was amazed that such a secret could be kept under lock and key from me for twenty-five-plus years, and I was mad with Daddy for never sharing any of this with me. Surely, he knew that one day, I would find out.

It took a chance meeting with Lavay McCullough and then Momma's conveyance of the story to change my life forever. As I contemplated the significance of what I had just learned on that hot August night in 1987, I made a pact within my own heart and mind that one day, when the time was right, I would seek to learn even more about this unbelievable story of my family's history.

In the weeks to follow after Momma's impactful revelation, I found it to be a difficult task setting aside all that I had come to learn about the lurid details of my family's history. The macabre actions taken by my grandfathers were paralyzing and mind-boggling. I struggled with my own identity as I toiled at putting their story out of my daily thoughts, and my own life as a young man. I felt as if I had a lot to live down. I pondered what, if any, of my grandfathers' mannerisms, characteristics and malevolent ways I had flowing through my veins. After all, they were one and two generations removed from me, and their Hulsey blood and DNA were present within me.

I had been told several years prior that I had inherited Granddaddy's mischievous ways. I thought of myself as a good and decent man. I had a good job at J.L. Lester & Son, where I enjoyed going to work each day. I was serving my second two-year term in Rockmart as a City Councilman, as an active member of the First Baptist Church, as an officer in the Rockmart Jaycees, and as a director of the Rockmart Little League.

Just like Daddy said I would be and how he had set the example for me to be, I was a positive contributor to the community. None of that mattered, particularly when I examined how Daddy had kept all of this a secret up to his death. As my struggles to overcome my family's past continued, my focus for the next few years turned to helping Momma and, eventually, to starting a new life away from my dear hometown of Rockmart.

When the time was right, I sensed the need to get away from the past and the anger that boiled inside of me due to Daddy's covertness. Residing within the confines of where the sinister acts wrought by my grandfather had occurred just didn't seem to be positive for me. I needed a change in my life and a change of venue for my residence was in order. After four years, that opportunity would come as a result of marriage.

On March 2, 1991, I married a former Rockmart resident and lifelong schoolmate and friend, Kelly Cummings Pitman. We had attended the same local schools from kindergarten up until our graduation from Rockmart High School in 1979. Both of our mothers enjoyed participating together in various community and social activities in Rockmart.

Growing up in Rockmart, Kelly was the daughter of Dr. T.E. (Ace) Cummings and Joan Cummings. The Cummings family had a prominent position within the community. In his physician's office, Ace was a partner with Dr. John Atha for most of his career. Everyone knew Ace and Joan by virtue of his caring for the physical needs of so many members of the community, and because of their active church, social, political, and benevolent activities within the community.

Kelly had previously been wed to Wesley Pitman, and together they had a son, Joseph. Prior to our nuptials, Kelly and I discussed where she, Joseph and I would reside once we had exchanged our wedding vows. I owned my home on Howard Street in Rockmart. I was in my fourth two-year term on the Rockmart City Council with a promising political career potentially ahead of me, and I had begun to rise in the ranks of the salesforce at J.L. Lester and Son.

Kelly and Joseph lived in the Country Walk subdivision of

Powder Springs. There was no need for two homes, and it seemed only natural that our home be in Rockmart, since that was our hometown and where her parents and siblings resided, as well as where Momma lived just right around the corner. As we mulled over the pros and cons of residing in either community, it became clear to us.

While, for me, Rockmart was the finest place a young boy could ever grow up, Powder Springs offered many more plusses than minuses. It was much closer to Piedmont Hospital in Atlanta, where Kelly worked, than it was from Rockmart and just about halfway between both of our workplaces. We also felt it would be in Joseph's, and any additional children we would be blessed with later, best interests to be in Powder Springs, particularly since the local schools (Varner Elementary, Tapp Middle and McEachern High) were, at that time, higher performing as those in Rockmart. Consequently, I would resign my City Council position and we would reside in Powder Springs.

While it didn't openly enter into our decision, it became an opportunity for me to get away from the place where the horrors of my grandfathers' wrongdoing had taken place so many years ago. Finally, at the age of twenty-nine, I would be starting my own family, away from Rockmart and all of the perceived trappings that came as a result of my family's horrid past.

At four-years-old, Joseph and I had already built a close relationship. His father, Wesley, loved Joseph in a very special way and has always allowed room for me in Joseph's life as his stepfather. I couldn't comprehend how

60 CENTS

Wesley must have felt as he had to begin sharing the duties of a father with another man – one that he knew very little about. For me, he became the quintessential father figure, one who loved Joseph enough to allow him to love me and for me to love and care for Joseph.

Wesley has never wavered from his commitment to support and encourage me as Joseph's stepfather. I, in turn, have always respected Wesley's rightful position as Joseph's father. He and I became good friends and have committed to make that last for as long as we live.

Only three months after our wedding, Kelly and I would learn that she was pregnant with our firstborn. Although it was supposed to be a surprise for me, I would deduce that this newborn was going to be a boy. Perhaps it was all of the baby blue clothing and baby accessories coming through our front door that gave it away. I was elated to be having a son. Now, I would have the awesome honor of having my own namesake and a child to carry on the Hulsey name.

On March 30, 1992, Evan Bradley Hulsey entered the world via Caesarean section at Piedmont Hospital. I was present during the birth, helpless and pretty much useless. The umbilical cord was wrapped around Evan's neck, and the physician's acted immediately to free it from him. When that concern was thwarted, the cord was severed.

A respiratory therapist took Evan from the delivering physician and was moving him to a position where he could perform routine measures performed during all births.

Suddenly, there appeared a stream of some sort of fluid that trajected upwardly toward the therapist's mask-covered face. Puzzled by what was taking place, I inquired of one of the nurses as to what was going on. She began laughing hysterically and said, "Your son is peeing all over the respiratory therapist!" I knew right then that this was my boy, already starting his own brand of mischief.

After attending to Evan, measuring and weighing him, placing a cap over his head and covering him with a warm blanket, our newborn son was placed in his mother's arms. All we could do was marvel at this precious, tiny human being in front of us.

The nurse asked if I wanted to hold Evan. I couldn't recall ever having held a baby before, but I nervously accepted the challenge and awesome responsibility of cuddling with my firstborn child. At that time, all I could do was gleam with pride as I held my son in my arms. He was a Hulsey, and he would eventually become the caretaker of the Hulsey name and all that it stands for.

As I began to consider the impact of his being born into the Hulsey family as Bill and Fred Hulsey Sr.'s great-great and great-grandson, it suddenly occurred to me that Evan would also potentially have a lot to live down. One day, I would have to tell him the history of his Hulsey lineage. As I had worked so fervently to put my grandfathers' actions and executions out of my mind for some time, the impact of what they had done and Daddy's subsequent cover-up would never leave my subconscious thoughts.

60 CENTS

Life events would continually stir up the memory of the Hulsey past and the secret kept from me. I vowed that, one day, I would tell my children about our family's heritage. I would not sweep it under the rug as Daddy had done. I would tell them what he didn't have the courage or strength to tell me. My indignation and frustration with Daddy increased each time I remembered all that had taken place back in the 1930s, and in knowing that he had hidden it all from me.

As we continued on in our lives working and raising a family, Kelly and I would experience ups and downs in our relationship that, years later, would lead to separation and, ultimately, divorce. But so much would transpire up until the demise of our union many years later. We were both solidly focused on our careers and raising two young boys. It would take most of our energy just to take on those two tasks. So, we thought, why not add one more to the Hulsey household?

Another blessing came to us on September 12, 1995, when our daughter, Rebecca Lane Hulsey, was born at Piedmont Hospital. Lane was without a doubt the most beautiful young lady I had ever laid eyes on. Once again, I was experiencing the awesome feeling of being a father and having a part in bringing new life into the world and into our family. What struck me the most, besides Lane's beauty and charm, was the fact that I had never been around little girls before. All at once, I was clueless to my duties and responsibilities of a father as it related to raising a girl.

I had been around only boys most of my home life, with Phil as my brother, and then Joseph and Evan as my sons. What in the world did I know about raising a daughter, except for my immediate "Rockmart redneck" reaction that I would shoot any boy that would come near my baby girl! I had to protect her, but I guess it was no joking matter to say that a Hulsey was going to shoot someone.

Several weeks afterward, when the excitement of new birth settled down to life's realities, the memories of the Hulsey family past stirred back up into my mind. Now, there was another child for me to explain her family's heritage to. I knew that, in time, it would only be right for me to share the story with both Evan and Lane, as well as Joseph. They had a right to know, just as I felt I had and deserved to hear it from Daddy.

The irony struck me how I felt that Daddy had let me down, and how Daddy's father had let him down, and how Daddy's father's father had let him down. I was determined that this all would stop with me and my children. No matter what, I would one day tell them the story of their Hulsey grandfathers.

Only two months after Lane was born, I was elected to the Powder Springs City Council. As I had done in Rockmart twelve years prior, I ran a grassroots campaign, walking door-to-door throughout the entirety of the city asking for the support and vote of the community. I garnered 60% of the vote against an incumbent council member who had lived his entire life in Powder Springs. The political life I had left in Rockmart had been revived in my new hometown of Powder Springs. I was sworn in and took office in January 1996.

A few months later, I would leave my position of Sales Manager at J.L. Lester and Son in Rockmart to start my own insurance business and career, with American Family Life and Assurance Company of Columbus, commonly referred to as AFLAC, headquartered in Columbus, Georgia. I went from a salaried position with benefits and a company-provided vehicle to a 100% commission job with no benefits, but with the potential of growing into an increased income, coupled with the freedom and flexibility of owning my own business.

By that time, Momma was seventy-years old and still living in Rockmart in the same house I had grown up in on Ivy Street. The kids and I would go visit her most every Sunday making the twenty-five-mile trek to and from Rockmart. By the time we arrived at home we would all be exhausted. At thirty-five-years-old, my plate was full with family, work and, as Daddy had said it would be, community service. There was very little room to spare in my day, and my thoughts would rarely stray back to all that I had learned about my Hulsey family some nine years prior.

The knowledge of what had taken place and the subsequent effects of the family history and Daddy's secretiveness never fully left me, however. It would linger around me like a scar from an old wound, occasionally providing a hint of pain and a reminder that it would never fully go away.

In 1999, after having completed a full, four-year term on the City Council, I ran unopposed for Mayor of Powder Springs, following in the huge footsteps of Powder Springs' longest-serving mayor and one of my greatest mentors, Richard D. Sailors. Richard had served four consecutive terms as Powder Springs' Mayor, totaling thirteen years. He remained a close friend and supporter of mine throughout and beyond my mayoral administration. Richard enjoyed ragging me in front of others for running without opposition. In his strong, gruff voice, he would exclaim, "Here I have had to run tireless and costly campaigns for mayor, and ole Brad just walks right in!" He was right, and it didn't bother me in the slightest. I would remark in jest to Richard that I ran unopposed because any potential candidates were too afraid to run against me. He would laugh at that premise.

Just as I was the youngest council member ever elected in Rockmart and Polk County, at the age of thirty-eight, I became the youngest mayor in Powder Springs' history. I learned very quickly that there was a vast difference serving on the City Council and in being Mayor.

There was much more demand on my time and, as Harry Truman once said about his presidency, "the buck stopped" at my desk when it came to responsibilities of and decisions to be made by the city government. I was in the spotlight, and I was expected to be the visionary leader of Powder Springs. I took my duties and responsibilities as Mayor seriously, and the eleven years I had spent as a City Councilman had helped prepare me to execute my office in a progressive, effective and caring manner.

60 CENTS

I was at the height of my community service that Daddy had prophesied about so many years ago. It was a great honor and privilege to serve as Mayor, but the thirty-plus hours I spent each and every week took its toll on my family life and my business. When I would visit the local schools, many of the children mused that I lived in a mayoral mansion with bodyguards, personal servants, chauffeur-driven limousines, a helicopter and jet airplane, and a million-dollar salary. Nothing could have been further from the truth, of course.

Along with the time I spent serving in my Mayoral capacity, I also had to work to support our family. My annual salary for serving as Mayor was $12,000.00, with no benefits. Most of my expenses were my responsibility, not the city's. Mind you, I knew all of this when I sought the position. But raising a family with three kids, a mortgage that had to be paid monthly along with all of the other bills and living expenses, operating an insurance business that demanded my full attention, and looking after an aging mother who lived alone in a town twenty-five miles away and, add to that, a full-time position as Mayor, left little time for quality family or personal time.

In June of 2003, almost three-and-a-half years into my first term in office as Mayor, I had made the decision to seek a second four-year term. There was unfinished business that I felt was important for me to lead the way toward making Powder Springs an even better place to raise a family and grow a business. As he would do from time to time, Evan joined me on one of my daily "drivearounds" through the city. I felt it my duty to look at projects that were taking place within the city limits, as well as at various concerns that had been shared with me by caring city staff and citizens. Evan was eleven years old, and I thought that this would provide the appropriate time for me to share my reelection plans with him.

As we rode down the streets and thoroughfares of our hometown, I gazed over at Evan in the passenger seat of my pickup truck. I could see clearly through his hazel-colored eyes to the outside of his window as I prepared to tell him the impending news. "Son", I offered, "Dad's term as Mayor ends this year. I've got a lot more to accomplish, so I've decided to seek another four-year term as Mayor. What do you think about that?"

Without directly looking at me, Evan murmured in his nasally and lisping voice, "That's great Dad. You'll do really good." Any parent who is worth half their weight in salt knows when their child is holding back saying more than they want. "What is it, son?", I asked. "What else do you want to share with me?"

As I pulled the truck over to focus on Evan, he looked back at me with quivering lips and a tear in his eyes and exclaimed, "I thought it would be cool if you and I could just hang out awhile." I felt as if I had been hit by a ton of bricks, but not in a bad way. Consequently, just like Evan, my lips began to quiver and tears came to my eyes when it all hit me at once. My son needed me, just like I had needed Daddy so many years ago.

Daddy had been so busy with all of his community activities that he hadn't stopped to watch my baseball games, to teach me how to fish, or to just sit on the front porch and talk childish nonsense amidst silly laughter with me. I was determined to be different, and I would be the father to Evan, Lane and Joseph that Daddy hadn't been for me. My priorities and focus changed toward my children at that very moment, and I decided that I would no longer be seeking a second term as Mayor.

After leaving the Mayor's office in January of 2004, I became solidly focused on my AFLAC career. I sought opportunities to grow my business through the legion of connections I had made as a result of my years of public service. I had worked hard at building meaningful and long-lasting relationships with the various governmental entities, service organizations, local business owners and community leaders I had come to know and admire.

The associations that came from working and serving with these good folks would go on to provide tremendous benefits in developing and enhancing my business and personal network, not to mention my income. Aside from the insurance business, I found myself engaged more and more with the children's activities.

Joseph and Evan were both involved in sports, primarily football. Joseph became an All-Cobb County tight end at McEachern High School, and then left home for the University of Tennessee-Chattanooga, where he played tight end for four years for the Mocs on a full scholarship.

Evan participated in the local Powder Springs Youth Football League. He would go on to play four years as a wide receiver on the Hawks football squad at one of Cobb County's newest schools, Hillgrove High School.

Lane began a ten-plus year cheerleading stint that began with the Powder Springs Youth Football League, and continued with competition cheerleading with the Stingray All-Stars, and football and competition cheerleading with the Hillgrove High Hawks. I would have the great honor of escorting Lane onto the football field as she represented her senior class on the Hillgrove homecoming court.

I did my best to be present for most of their games and competitions, and in volunteering my time and finances in supporting the needs of their respective organizations. It was such a thrill to be a part of their lives and to enjoy watching them grow and mature as they participated in the activities they loved.

I eventually told the children about our grandfathers' murders and executions. Naturally, they were shocked that this was a part of their family's heritage. Being young people with more on their minds than grisly family tales, they accepted what I told them but, unlike me, decided not to dwell over what had occurred so many years ago.

As I gave as much of my time to growing and nurturing the children, I found that I had no time to research my family's history. While important to me, it would continue to stay on the backburner, but never completely out of my thoughts.

With my precious children, from l to r: Lane, me, Evan and Joseph.

CHAPTER ELEVEN:
"I AM STILL A PERSON"

With all of the busyness and constraints that came with family and business life, I still made it a point to visit Momma at her home in Rockmart as often as I could. On most Sunday afternoons after church I, usually along with one or more of the children, would make the twenty-five-mile one-way trek to my dear hometown to check on Momma and to assist her with any needs she might have. She was now in her late seventies, and had years earlier adjusted well to living alone.

By now, Momma was no "spring chicken," and she needed my help with certain duties around her house. She made it known that she would not consider leaving her beautiful brick home with the slate roof on it and that in no manner of thinking would she consider moving into a smaller, more manageable living environment.

As for me, I thought it would be nice to have Momma move closer to our home in Powder Springs, primarily because it would allow me to spend more time with her and to better look after her needs. Phil and his wife, Deborah, were firmly rooted in their home in Columbia, Tennessee, a good four hours away from Rockmart. They had moved there several years prior when, after being laid off from the General Motors assembly plant in Doraville, Georgia, Phil accepted a position at the Saturn automobile assembly plant located in nearby Spring Hill, Tennessee.

60 CENTS

My subtle pleas to get Momma to sell her home and move closer to us in Powder Springs would continually fall on deaf ears. She was not going to leave her place of comfort – her home of over forty-four years. As far as she was concerned, there would be no discussion of the matter – case closed.

On most of our visits to Momma's, we usually made it a point to spend an hour or two at Aunt Dossie's and Uncle Willie's house. Since Evan and Lane had never known either one of their grandfathers, Uncle Willie had over the years become somewhat of a surrogate grandfather to them. They affectionately called him "Papa," and Uncle Willie delighted in them calling him by that moniker. Evan and Lane relished the opportunity to play with their "Papa," and their total focus would be on him as soon as we arrived at their home on Prospect Road in Rockmart.

As 2005 rolled around, it was becoming apparent that something wasn't right about Uncle Willie. His high-spirited, fun-loving personality was changing to a more subdued aura, and he appeared to be somewhat distant from the kids and everyone else around him. He soon became forgetful, continuously misplacing his wallet, keys and other personal belongings. His words became slurred and incomprehensible. He would constantly blow air out of the side of his lips that would resemble the sound of a horse's whinny. All of us knew something just wasn't normal about our beloved Willie.

After a visit with his local doctor and, ultimately, a neurologist in Rome, Georgia, Uncle Willie would be diagnosed with Alzheimer's, a progressive disease that destroys memory and other important mental functions. Aunt Dossie, along with their two daughters and my first cousins, Jane and Freda, and their families did all they could to make Uncle Willie's life as ordinary as possible.

Uncle Willie was a large and imposing figure, standing tall at six-feet, six-inches, and weighing over 250 pounds. At times, due to the dread disease, he would unknowingly become uncontrollable with fits of anger and frustration. He would see his own reflection in a mirror or window and was convinced that an intruder was attempting to do harm to Aunt Dossie and him.

Many times, Uncle Willie would sneak out of the house when Aunt Dossie would be busy with household chores or taking care of her own personal needs. On countless occasions, passersby would find Uncle Willie walking down the busy and narrow Prospect Road there in Rockmart. He would have no clue where he was or what he was doing. As most of the good people of the community already knew Uncle Willie, and as they were wont to do, they would kindly offer him a ride home.

It would take all of Aunt Dossie's and their family's attention and energy to tend to Uncle Willie. To watch the love and care that poured out from the family toward him was heartwarming and provided an example to me that I would soon come to replicate in my own life.

As the Alzheimer's disease progressed and pushed Uncle Willie more and more away from normalcy, he would eventually be diagnosed with another dread disease, one that Daddy had faced some ten years prior. Colon cancer had taken hold of him, and Aunt Dossie and her family faced a daunting decision – what would they do about the cancer in the midst of dealing with Uncle Willie's Alzheimer's?

The situation was strenuous and more than most families could handle. Aunt Dossie, Jane, Freda and the rest of the family were strong in their conviction to provide love and care to Uncle Willie. Together, they would make the difficult decision to not treat the cancer, and to continue their care for Uncle Willie at home.

Jane and Freda, along with Freda's daughters, Michelle and Melody (my second cousins), would take turns spending the night to assist Aunt Dossie with Uncle Willie. It would take all of them working together to see after Uncle Willie's needs. They were faithful to the challenges they faced ahead. It would be an arduous task for them, but they loved Uncle Willie and had faith and trust in themselves as a family, and in the Good Lord above.

****

On one particular morning in late 2005, I made a business call on several new employees at the City of Rockmart, one of my valued AFLAC accounts. As I typically did when I was in Rockmart on business, I phoned Momma to let her know I would be dropping by afterward to visit and eat a sandwich with her for lunch. It had been almost two weeks since I had seen her, and I missed my dear mother.

Normally, Momma would have greeted this news with excitement, but this time was different than any before. "Couldn't you have given me a little more notice?", she asked. "I'm not dressed, I haven't been to the grocery store in several days, and I don't have anything for you to eat here!"

I was taken aback by Momma's assertive and pointed behavior, and I knew that something wasn't right. Once I finished my presentation to the City employees, I hurried over to Momma's to see what the problem was. Upon arriving and entering my old homeplace there on Ivy Street, I saw that the usually tidy house was cluttered, disarranged, and rather dusty. This was very uncharacteristic of Momma's housekeeping. I found Momma standing in her kitchen, still dressed in her housecoat and pajamas, even though it was 12:30 in the afternoon. She was feverishly stirring something up in the old peach-colored mixing bowl she had used for years solely for making cornbread in.

I could see on the kitchen counter an empty can of tuna, a jar of sweet pickle relish, and a half-used package of cream cheese. Momma was obviously agitated with me as I approached to hug her, something I had been doing for over forty-four years. As she backed away from my attempt to put my arms around her, she looked up at me with tears flowing down her face. I gently took the mixing bowl out of her hands and sat it down on the counter.

I lovingly rubbed Momma's hands as she began sobbing uncontrollably. I pulled her close to me and stroked her disheveled hair as I whispered to her that everything was going to be okay. She was seventy-nine years old, and as I held her next to me, I became distraught at the thought of what could be wrong. I knew I needed to pull myself together and to be calm for Momma. I assured her that everything was just fine, and that I was so glad that I could stop by to visit and have lunch with her.

Wiping away her tears, Momma nervously continued preparation of what was supposed to be tuna salad. As I opened the old two-door refrigerator to get us something to drink, I saw on one of the side shelves a full, unopened jar of mayonnaise. This was the usual condiment that Momma would use in her tuna salad, not cream cheese.

After Momma spread the suspicious salad onto two slices of wheat bread, she handed the sandwich to me on a paper plate. I thanked her and squeezed her noticeably trembling hands in a show of love and appreciation. I held back any comments as I held my breath and bit into the tuna and cream cheese sandwich, acting as if I was thoroughly enjoying it.

The fishy taste of the tuna, along with the sweet flavor of the pickle relish and the slightly sour and salty cream cheese made for an unusual and interesting sensation to my taste buds. The texture of the mix was heavy, with a consistency thicker than butter. Putting my best effort forward in an attempt to calm Momma, I pretended to be enjoying my lunch, smiling as I chewed and choked down the sandwich. All the while, I pondered Momma's obvious changed condition and to what may lie ahead.

As I left Momma's home that afternoon, I immediately phoned both Phil and Aunt Dossie to inform them of the condition of Momma's house, her radical behavior, and of the "tuna salad" she had made for lunch. Just as I was, Phil was concerned over Momma's uncommon behavior. I promised my brother I would keep a close eye on Momma. Phil, as he always did, extended me support and encouragement as I did my best to look out for Momma's best interests. He offered to come down from Tennessee to assist me. I graciously declined and told him I would call him immediately if I felt his presence was needed.

Aunt Dossie had visited Momma only a couple of days prior to my visit. She had observed a difference in Momma that reminded her of Uncle Willie at the onset of his Alzheimer's diagnosis. Aunt Dossie urged me to have Momma see a doctor at once. I heeded her remarks and immediately phoned Momma's local primary physician. The doctor's office staff promptly scheduled an appointment for Momma to see a neurologist at the Harbin Clinic in nearby Rome, Georgia. Unfortunately, it would be almost a month-and-a-half before the neurologist's office had an open appointment. After receiving a return phone call from her primary care physician's office, I turned my car around and went back to Momma's house.

It had been close to one hour since I had departed. Upon arriving, I walked into the den and found Momma sitting in her easy chair with no lights or the television on. She was still in her housecoat and pajamas, her wide-open crystal blue eyes staring with a faraway look at the space in front of her. It was as if she was in a trance.

60 CENTS

I gently stroked the back of her head to arouse her. As she came to, she let out a groan of despair. I asked her what was the matter, and she exclaimed nothing was wrong. I knew better. I would stay with her throughout the rest of the day and into the evening, returning home to Powder Springs and the family only after I was assured Momma was okay and resting comfortably in bed.

It wasn't easy for me to leave her all alone. As I departed, and unbeknownst to her, I took Momma's car keys out of her purse. I had made the tough decision that she should no longer drive. I would learn several weeks later from some of the townspeople that Momma had on more than one occasion driven in the wrong direction on Marble Street in downtown Rockmart, a one-way thoroughfare. The odd thing is – Momma never asked me what happened to her car keys.

I was desperate to determine Momma's condition. My senses told me she had Alzheimer's, but I certainly was not trained and had no medical knowledge of what was taking place. I performed extensive research regarding Momma's behavior. From that, I would determine that, at the least, she was suffering from senile dementia and, at the most, Alzheimer's Disease.

Aunt Dossie's hands were full with caring for Uncle Willie. I couldn't ask her to look after Momma as she tended to Uncle Willie's needs. I called on several of Momma's neighbors and the Rockmart First Baptist Church family to help keep a watch over her and, to no surprise, they were very willing to oblige.

Momma's next-door neighbor, Bernice Payne, would brew a pot of coffee and invite Momma to come over to sit a spell and enjoy a fresh cup. Usually it was during the middle of the afternoon, and Bernice would call to let me know how Momma was doing. By now, Mary Lumpkin had passed away, but her husband, William still lived at their home on Ivy Street. William would generously make the trek through his and Bernice's backyards to Momma's back door, knocking until Momma would finally open up for him to visit.

On many occasions, both Bernice and William would share their evening's supper with Momma. Many from Momma's church family would drop by or call to check on her. Jimmy Lester, my dear friend and boss from my J.L. Lester & Son years, would be dependable in visiting Momma, as would many, many others. When she was able to catch a break, Aunt Dossie would take time out to see about her sister.

****

Since I was knee-high to a grasshopper and could remember, it had been a family tradition to visit Aunt Dossie's and Uncle Willie's home for Christmas supper and gift-giving on Christmas Eve. On Christmas Eve 2005, the kids and I stopped by Momma's house to pick her up. Momma's contribution toward the feast was to be some type of dessert. She had already informed me that she would be preparing one of her scrumptious caramel cakes. The delectable homemade caramel icing recipe was passed down to Momma from her grandmother, Fannie Williams, who was affectionately known in our family as "Ma"

60 CENTS

Williams. Maw Maw Holland had used the same recipe for years. The instructions seemed basic, but there appeared to be something extraneous to Momma's blend of ingredients that set her caramel icing apart and above others that I have tasted. Simply put, with no prejudice, Momma's was the best.

As the kids and I strolled into Momma's tiny kitchen, it was déjà vu all over again. I could see that she had the sheet cake baked and ready for frosting, but there was no icing to be seen. We were supposed to be at Aunt Dossie's at 5:30 p.m., and it was already 5:10 p.m. Momma was, once again, uncharacteristically stirring up something other than cornbread in the peach-colored mixing bowl. It was the caramel icing, and I had never witnessed her stirring it so briskly in the past.

I told Momma it was about time for us to leave, and she immediately became agitated. I should have known better to have said something, given the perceived neurological state I believed her to be in.

Suddenly, from out of nowhere it seemed, Momma opened a can of coconut and instantaneously dumped the contents into the bowl of icing. Never before was their coconut called for or added to the caramel icing. Momma continued on as if nothing was different. Once the coconut was uniformly blended with the icing, Momma hurriedly spread the mixture evenly over the yellow sheet cake. Bewildered by what had just occurred, the kids and I looked at each other with confusion and exasperation.

How could she have ruined such a fine confection by adding coconut to it? As Momma covered up the caramel-coconut cake, we rushed out the front door, the time being 5:35 p.m. No doubt, it was past time to have Momma examined by the neurologist. The icing fiasco was another episode of an evolving theory – Momma probably had Alzheimer's Disease.

After arriving twenty minutes late, we all sat down and enjoyed our delicious Christmas Eve meal at Aunt Dossie's and Uncle Willie's. Freda helped Uncle Willie prepare his plate. I would prepare Momma's for her. I had forewarned everyone about the caramel-coconut cake. When it came time for dessert, I decided to be the "guinea pig" and be the first to taste the cake. There were other desserts, including homemade pecan pie, but I didn't want to hurt Momma's feelings.

I was stunned as I sank my fork down into the creamy, moist caramel-coconut "surprise" and crammed it into my mouth. Even with all of her mishaps in preparing the cake, Momma had once again hit a culinary homerun. The caramel and the coconut made a tasty combination, and everyone enjoyed a piece of Momma's "special" recipe.

****

As 2006 rolled around, it came time for Momma's appointment with the neurologist. I picked her up early so that we could enjoy lunch at one of her favorite local restaurants in Rome, Duffy's Deli. Selfishly, I didn't want to burden Momma to the point that she would prepare another bowl of her "tuna salad".

60 CENTS

Once we arrived at the Harbin Clinic, we checked in and eventually were called back to the exam room. The neurologist entered with a hearty hello and a pat on Momma's back. Momma was sitting on the exam table with her legs freely swinging back and forth under it. From the grin on her face, I could tell that she thought the neurologist was handsome.

After I explained some of Momma's symptoms, variations in life patterns and cooking episodes, the neurologist began asking Momma a series of questions. "What is today, Mrs. Hulsey?" Momma answered correctly, "Well, it's Thursday, of course." "Good! Good!", the neurologist exclaimed. "Now Mrs. Hulsey, please tell me who the current President of the United States is." Momma dropped her head and then looked up to me for assistance. I told her she was on her own for that question. She thought for a while, looked at the neurologist with a smile and said, "I don't know his name, but I sure do like him!"

For the record, the U.S. President at that time was George W. Bush. The neurologist continued to interrogate Momma with several simple, straightforward questions that she should have easily known the answer to. Sadly, she couldn't answer most of them.

The neurologist backed himself up into a corner of the exam room. Looking down and then up at me with a concerned look on his young face, the neurologist uttered the words that I had suspected, but wasn't prepared to hear.

"Mr. Hulsey, your mother has Alzheimer's Disease." He went on, "Mrs. Hulsey, I'm sorry to share this news with you. There are tests we need to run, including a scan of your brain. And there are some medications we will need to start you on immediately to help you deal with this disease." Momma didn't appear to understand the magnitude of the diagnosis that had just been shared with us.

Leaving the exam room, the neurologist pulled me aside and said, "Mr. Hulsey, these medications your mother will be taking will not cure her of this disease. They will only help to prolong the inevitable, which is a deterioration of the brain function and ultimately, if other causes don't take her first, death. You should consider placing her in a care home of some sort, or have a full-time sitter at her home." I was astounded as we left the clinic. I didn't know what was in store for Momma's future and how it would impact mine.

After Momma's Alzheimer's diagnosis, it took eight long, grueling months for Phil and me to convince Momma it was time for her to get out of the large, ten-room house on Ivy Street and to move into smaller, more manageable living quarters. The truth of the matter is that we didn't actually convince her, we just stirred her thoughts. It had to be her decision, and after spending too many lonely nights in her den staring at the walls, and after leaving a pot of green beans on the stove until they caught fire, Momma came to the conclusion it was time to vacate the place she had called home for forty-four years.

Only a couple of days after her realization, I took Momma to visit two assisted living facilities nearby our home in Powder Springs. She and I both agreed on one facility in particular as being cozy, well-kept and, after sampling the food, that would provide her with the best quality meals she could want. We signed a contract with an assisted living facility on Powder Springs Road, where we would be moving Momma into her one-room living quarters in less than two weeks.

As we traveled back to Rockmart, Momma seemed content that she had made her own decision about her living arrangements. I didn't sense any remorse or regrets in her tone or stature. As for me, this would bring her closer for me to look in on her more frequently, to know that she was in a safe and caring environment, and that would allow Phil and me the opportunity to dispose of the house in Rockmart and most of Momma's belongings while she was alive. Both Phil and I agreed that this made things much easier than to have to deal with these issues after Momma had passed away.

Phil, his wife, Deborah and I would move Momma into the assisted living facility in September 2006. Eventually, she would find peace and a sense of belonging with her new surroundings and the other residents she cohabitated with.

****

In January 2009, Uncle Willie would succumb to the devastating effects of both Alzheimer's and cancer. With

Aunt Dossie's and the family's support, he had waged a valiant and gruesome battle against both of these terrible diseases. Aunt Dossie was exhausted from the months of caretaking she and her girls had so unselfishly provided to Uncle Willie. They would clean him, dress him, provide him with water and an occasional sip of his favorite soft drink. For weeks before his death, he could no longer eat, but he did like sucking on a Tootsie Pop.

They had painstakingly attended to Uncle Willie's every need. And then, although not unexpected, he was gone. He was now at rest in Heaven.

At Uncle Willie's funeral, his granddaughter, Melody offered a heartfelt eulogy to her "Papa". She shared beautiful memories of days gone by, when Uncle Willie was at the top of his game, making all of us feel loved and admired. A big part of all of our lives was now missing with the death of Willie Hardy.

****

Momma was in no condition to attend Uncle Willie's funeral. Even though she was maintaining much of the wit and feistiness that had always characterized her, her mental condition was slowly worsening. Eventually, she would be moved to the Alzheimer's wing of the assisted living facility where she could receive much more attentive care. She remained able to walk about the confines of the locked Alzheimer's area, and she enjoyed the closer, more intense care provided to her by the facility staff.

60 CENTS

All of that would change forever. On Father's Day of 2010, Momma and I were walking to my car with a plan to drive over to the local Starbucks for a cup of coffee, an adventure we would take many times during her time at the facility. I was carrying Momma's dirty laundry basket in both of my hands as she walked behind me.

Suddenly, I heard Momma shriek with fear, and I heard a loud thump. Turning around, I saw Momma lying on the pavement, a crimson-colored pool forming while blood gushed from her mouth and head. She had taken a nasty and life-altering spill onto the drive near the entrance to the facility. I dropped the laundry and quickly ran inside to call for assistance.

The caretakers at the facility moved swiftly out of the front door and toward Momma. One of them had already phoned 9-1-1 for emergency assistance. Momma was on the ground, out cold. One of her teeth had broken and was situated next to her hemorrhaging mouth. When the ambulance arrived, they checked Momma's vital signs and determined that her heart rate and blood pressure were elevated, but not to overly dangerous levels. The medics attended to her wounds, moved her limp body onto the gurney, and then loaded her into the ambulance.

They told me that they were taking her to the emergency room at Cobb Hospital in Marietta. As the rear doors of the emergency vehicle were shut with a loud clang, and with red lights flashing and the siren blaring, Momma would leave the assisted living facility for the last time.

After days of convalescing and healing at Cobb Hospital, Momma's mental state would rapidly decline. The attending physician said that the fall and subsequent injuries, coupled with a total state of confusion brought about by a sudden change in scenery and in her physical condition, had exacerbated the effects of her Alzheimer's Disease. She would need total attention to her physical needs that were not offered by the assisted living facility.

As I looked into her loving, yet wayward eyes, I could sense Momma trying to tell me something. She could only mumble vacuous words and phrases; however, there still remained emotion in her countenance. I felt as if Momma was conveying the message, "Please do not forget, Son, I am still a person."

With Phil's support and blessings, I made the decision to move Momma into the Powder Springs Nursing and Rehabilitation Home, located near downtown Powder Springs. It would be close enough to our house so that I could take care of her in her new surroundings.

Momma was bound to living out her remaining years in the nursing home. She would no longer enjoy the "creature comforts" of her own bed, easy chair and other furnishings she had brought from her Rockmart home to the assisted living facility.

I made a promise to our family and, most importantly, to God that I would do all within my ability to see to Momma's well-being, just as I had when she moved into the assisted living facility. I wanted to maintain her dignity as much as was possible. Always engrained into my soul, however, was the need to learn more about the family secret that had been revealed to me by Momma more than seventeen years prior. I promised myself that I would not let go of my desire to one day discover more of the truth about what had taken place so long ago.

Uncle Willie and Aunt Dossie having fun with Evan.

CHAPTER TWELVE: DARK HAPPENS

Aside from Momma's permanent confinement in the nursing home, 2010 also brought about many challenges and life-altering experiences that exceeded my wildest dreams. Every fabric of my body, spirit, soul and mind would be tested in ways I would never wish upon my worst enemy and, most assuredly, myself.

The mountaintop highs and the valley lows that would come my way that year would forever transform the manner in which I interacted with my family and friends, and with how I coped with so many life situations that, in the past, I couldn't have dealt with appropriately. Consequently, I would find a renewed spirit and energy toward my quest in learning more about Granddaddy and Great-Granddaddy Hulsey, the atrocious murders they committed, and their subsequent trial and eventual executions.

As 2010 dawned, Evan and I were excited to be planning our second trip to the Czech Republic, slated for early July. In 2009 we, at the urging of my close and trusted friend, Randy Hardy, joined him, his sons Jake and Sam, and several other members of our church family from McEachern Memorial United Methodist on a mission trip to the Czech Republic. We, as the "American Team," partnered with members of our sister Methodist church from Jihlava, Czech Republic, in leading and instructing a large contingent of Czech teenagers at Youth English Camp.

The camp was held in the tiny village of Daňkovice, a breathtaking, mountainous community located in the country's Vysočina Region, approximately a two-hour drive from the Czech capital of Prague. The basic premise of the camp was for the American and Czech leadership teams to serve together in teaching English to the Czech students through classroom learning, dramatic and musical activities, athletic competition, and all-day fellowship.

While openly professing our Christian beliefs was not a primary element of the camp, we were allowed to teach English via reading from the Holy Bible. At that time, the Czech Republic was ranked as the second-most atheistic country in the world. If a Czech student wanted to learn more about our Christian faith and beliefs, we were free to discuss it with them. We were specifically instructed to not force our beliefs on anyone that was not receptive to hearing them, and we honored those instructions.

Initially, Evan and I were somewhat cool to the thought of participating in the 2009 camp. Those feelings changed once we experienced the blessings that unfolded as we served together alongside our respective teams. We forged meaningful lifetime relationships with many of the Czech youths and leaders.

We couldn't wait to return to serve God at the 2010 Youth English Camp, and to once again spend time with our Czech brothers and sisters. I was tapped by our Missions team at McEachern Methodist to be the American leader for the upcoming trip, an honor I was humbled and grateful to have bestowed upon me. In January 2010 I began forming a team and making plans for our journey of service slated for July 2010.

****

For months, I had been experiencing pain in my lower back. It began as a mild twinge that would fester occasionally and then suddenly subside. I thought nothing of it until, over a couple of weeks, the pain began to intensify and linger, up to a point where it was so excruciating that I would be drawn to tears. It felt as if someone had thrust a sharp dagger into my back and then began twisting it into my spine. I knew that something wasn't right, and I needed my primary care physician to examine me and determine what the problem was exactly.

After having x-rays taken of my lower back, my physician diagnosed me as having a bulging disc in the very lowest area of my spine. He suggested physical therapy and pain medications as needed to treat the infirmity. I would do as suggested, and limited my intake of the medications to only when the pain was too severe to handle.

The therapy didn't appear to be helping as my condition worsened. By late January, I beseeched my physician to explore other possibilities with my deteriorating physical health. He suggested I make an appointment with a neurosurgeon who specialized in spinal conditions.

60 CENTS

Before I would actually meet with the neurosurgeon, he ordered a magnetic resonance imaging (MRI) test of my lower back and spine. It was torturous for me to lie still on the table as the MRI was performed. I knew the neurosurgeon needed the images to determine what was causing my debilitation, so I was a willing participant in the test. It had gotten more and more difficult for me to sleep, bathe, dress and perform daily tasks. I needed relief from my misery.

The MRI took place on a snowy Friday afternoon, and I would have to wait for three of the longest days of my life to receive the diagnosis and subsequent treatment plan from the neurosurgeon. Naturally, I hoped and prayed for a positive outcome.

The following Monday, I had scheduled an AFLAC enrollment at a local Chick Fil-A restaurant near our home. I didn't know exactly when I would be hearing from the neurosurgeon's office, so I decided to go ahead with the enrollment, even though I physically and mentally wasn't up to working. Perhaps going about my daily routine would help keep my mind off of the suffering I was enduring, and it would help pass the time away as I awaited the news on my condition.

That morning, as I was driving to the Chick Fil-A for their enrollment meeting, my cell phone suddenly rang. Having entered the phone number into my contacts earlier, I saw immediately that it was the neurosurgeon's office. As I nervously answered the call, I was surprised to hear the physician's voice. "Mr. Hulsey," he softly uttered. "I am calling you to ask if you can come into my office today?"

I could tell by the tone of the neurosurgeon's voice that something was amiss. Why did he want me to come into his office? Couldn't he tell me right then what was going on? I implored him to tell me what he had discovered about my back from the MRI results. Hesitantly, he complied with my wishes.

The neurosurgeon spoke in a melancholy tone, "Mr. Hulsey, I've taken a long look at the results of your MRI. I have conferred with several of my colleagues. I'm sorry, but it appears that you have a mass at the base of your spine that, I believe, is cancerous." My vehicle was idled at a traffic light across from our church home, McEachern Methodist, as I heard those devastating words.

Overcome with a myriad of emotions, I was speechless as the neurosurgeon continued. "As I stated earlier, I think you should come to my office today so that we can discuss this further. I'm so sorry to have to share this news over the phone with you. Do you think you can come in?" In a state of shock from the news that I had cancer, I whispered to him that I would be there later. As the light turned green, I accelerated my vehicle and quickly turned into the church parking lot.

Entering the church offices, oblivious to the pain in my spine, I hurriedly walked upstairs and into the open door of our Associate Pastor, Charlie Marus. Charlie knew something wasn't right, and he pulled up a chair for me to

60 CENTS

sit in. As I adjusted my body in the chair to a position that was as close to comfortable as could be, I began to unload my story of despair on Charlie. Without hesitation, Charlie paged the other two clergy members who were present in the church at that time; Donna Goff, our Missions Pastor, and Allen Richburg, our Evangelism Pastor.

After telling them the harrowing news of my apparent cancer diagnosis, Charlie anointed my head with oil that Allen had gotten from his office. They then laid their hands upon my head as each one of them offered a prayer of comfort and healing for me. I knew I had to get home and then to the neurosurgeon's office, so I thanked them for their concern and care, hugged each of them, and then left with tears flowing down my cheeks.

I soon headed to the neurosurgeon's office located nearby Piedmont Hospital in Atlanta. Upon arriving, I was immediately escorted to where the neurosurgeon awaited. He began to show me the images that distinctly showed a mass on my lower spine. The area was dark and had no clarity, while the rest of my spine appeared clear and normal. He surmised that, while there was a very remote chance this could be some sort of infection, the mass was cancerous in nature and, given its location on the spine, inoperable.

With a solemn, grievous look on his face, the neurosurgeon suggested that I, "Go home and get your affairs in order. We will call you back in to see me once, after consultation with other physicians, we determine the best course of action to take to help keep you as comfortable as possible."

My head dropped in grief, sorrow and disbelief when I heard those words. What about my family? They were counting on me. I had a responsibility to be around for them, to provide for them, to protect them. I longed to travel back to the Czech Republic with Evan, and had made a commitment to the McEachern Methodist team and, most importantly, to God to lead us that summer. What was I going to do?

The children were young. Joseph had just turned twenty-three, Evan would soon be turning eighteen and Lane was fourteen. The boys were, of course, saddened by the news. They showed themselves as strong young men as they did their best to hold themselves together for my benefit.

Lane, on the other hand, couldn't hold back her emotions. When she and I first saw each other after receiving the devastating news, Lane rushed into my arms and held me as close as she could. I could feel both of our hearts pounding as she clutched me tightly, all the while wailing and lamenting her grief over the prospect of losing her Daddy.

As my heart was breaking for Lane, I did my best to console her, holding her for what seemed an eternity. I wanted to keep her safe from the heartbreak she was suffering, but I couldn't. It was undoubtedly one of the most difficult times of my life.

After three restless nights at home, I could no longer stand the pain. I was admitted into Piedmont Hospital, where they administered intravenous pain medications and, soon after, performed a battery of tests on my spine, including a biopsy and a CT scan. When the on-call neurologist returned with my test results he addressed me.

"Mr. Hulsey, I have good news for you, and I have bad news for you. Which do you want first?" All of the news over the past several days had sapped most of the vitality within me, so if there was a hint of something positive on the horizon, I needed to hear it first.

Still groggy from the pain medications, I muttered, "Give me the good news, Doc." The doctor responded, "Okay then, the good news is you don't have inoperable cancer. Actually, you don't have cancer at all." I thought, "Did I hear what I think I just heard?" In a split second, all of the anguish I had experienced over the worries of dealing with the cancer had been relieved.

I couldn't believe what the doctor had just shared, but I was grateful to God for sparing me from cancer. Still, I knew that there was some negative account left to come. The doctor continued, "The bad news is you have a severe staph infection on your spine. It will require large intravenous doses of antibiotics that will take months to rid you of the infection, as well as pain management drugs. We will begin the regimen here in the hospital for several days, and then send you home for a long period of recuperation and restoration."

I wanted to jump out of the bed and celebrate with dancing over the news I had just heard. I was in no shape to do so.

My family and friends were cautiously overjoyed with the report that I didn't have inoperable cancer. The tables had turned, and I now had a renewed verve about me, although my weakened, tormented body wouldn't allow me to get up and rejoice. I vowed to follow all of the doctor's instructions so that I would be restored to full health or, at least, a new-normal way of life.

For the life of me, I have no clue how a staph infection got internally into my spine. Nevertheless, I was determined to fight it off. Doing so would be a long and arduous task. I needed to get well. I had a responsibility to take care of and provide for my family's needs. I was responsible for seeing after Momma's well-being. I still wanted to lead the American team to Youth English Camp in the Czech Republic. The doctor made no promise to me as to whether my condition would warrant my going abroad. Only time would tell.

I would be admitted into Piedmont Hospital twice during the ordeal for a total of twelve days. In spite of the narcotics I was receiving along with the antibiotics, the rigorous pain I was subjected to by the staph infection was over-whelming. The stress and strain of lying on my back constantly for twenty-four hours was grueling. Subsequently, I began experiencing an irregular and very fast heart rate or, medically speaking, atrial fibrillation.

The doctors theorized the atrial fibrillation was probably manifested from the immense negative stress my body was enduring, coupled with my genetic hypertension that I had continuously been treated for since I was twenty-one years old. A group of cardiologists had to be brought in to treat the heart condition. If left untreated, atrial fibrillation could cause stroke, heart failure and other heart-related complications. I was prescribed an anti-arrhythmic drug, a blood thinner and placed on a heart monitor.

I felt like a professional sports franchise owner who had drafted my own "team", but instead of professional athletes, this squad consisted of health care personnel. The lineup consisted of my dedicated primary care physician, cardiologists for the atrial fibrillation, neurologists and infectious disease doctors for the staph infection in my spine, pain management specialists, and the finest group of caring nurses, nurse assistants, radiologists and other hospital personnel. Together, we were confident that we would eventually thwart the distressing circumstances my body was experiencing.

I would learn that people all over the globe, an extended part of the "team", including my dear friends in the Czech Republic, were praying for my recovery. I owed it to God, my family, and the host of prayer warriors to fight with all the vigor I could muster to overcome my dilapidated physical state.

I was allowed to go home once the cardiologists were able to get the atrial fibrillation under control and my heart back into normal sinus rhythm. A peripherally inserted central catheter or "PICC" line, a long, thin, hollow tube, was placed into a vein in my right arm to help me administer the four-times daily dosages of antibiotics into my infectious body. Patches were prescribed for my back that would help alleviate the agonizing pain I was feeling in my lower spinal area. I was in a weakened condition, having lost more than thirty pounds, and suffering from muscle atrophy due to my lack of physical activity.

Disabled by the pain and infection and unable to work, I would spend three long and lonely months recuperating at home. Most days, I would sit and stare at the walls in total silence, wondering if anyone would come to see me. I did have many caring family members and friends come and visit me while convalescing at home, delivering food, magazines and other items to help out and hopefully cheer me up.

There were so many friends I wanted to see or hear from that would never come to see about me. I understand that most of us live busy and hectic lives, but I was saddened and disconcerted that many of my friends, for whatever their reasons, didn't take the time to call, send a note of encouragement, or pay a visit.

Subsequent to my loneliness and despair, I would experience depression far beyond my imagination, something I never dreamed I would ever encounter. When I could sleep, I would have outlandish dreams about having walls close in on me, of demons lurking outside my bedroom window readying themselves to pounce on me, and of dying all alone. To say that my life was in a pit would be an understatement. I was just about at my wits end.

Finally, after three agonizing months, the severe pain in my back began dissipating. Still, my psyche was at its lowest point ever. I had endured the roughest and most strenuous physical and emotional battle of my life. Although I had my family and some friends around me throughout the calamity, I continued to experience loneliness and depression.

****

It was spring of 2010, and the much-anticipated Czech Youth English Camp was on the horizon. The American team I had been tapped to lead had continued on in its planning and preparation without me there to guide them. As it has been said, "the show must go on". They had done yeoman's work in preparing for the eventual journey. My doctors cleared me for travel, and my teammates readily accepted me back as not just one of them, but as their leader. It seemed a miracle to me that I would get to return to the Czech Republic, and with Evan by my side.

Only a couple of weeks before our departure to Prague, Associate Pastor Charlie Marus filled the pulpit at McEachern Methodist in our Senior Pastor's, Jim Higgins, absence. The sermon title for that Sunday morning was "Dark Happens". I opined to myself that Charlie would be talking about the dark financial days our country had been experiencing over the past two years as a result of the housing bubble and recession that began in 2008.

As he progressed into his discourse, I sensed that Charlie was preaching to me. In fact, it was God using Charlie as His communicator and teacher to speak directly to my heart at a time when I needed it most.

In his sermon, Charlie spoke of how we as humans will, at some time in our lives, experience difficult circumstances where we reach the lowest of our lows. It could be through the death of a loved one, a serious illness or injury, divorce, bankruptcy...there can be so many ways our lives may become closed-in where no light can shine through, and we experience dreadful, lonely and dark days.

During the darkest of my days dealing with the incorrect diagnosis and the subsequent battle with the staph infection and atrial fibrillation, I sometimes questioned why God had allowed this to happen to me. Charlie would help set the record straight for me as he continued sharing the message.

Charlie proclaimed, "As dark does happen in our lives from time to time, it is not as if God has placed a curse on us or caused whatever brought about the darkness to occur. It is, however, through that darkness, and through our experiences of despair and woe that God uses those situations to open our eyes, hearts and minds to the wonder of all the glorious things He can do as He guides us through the darkness and into His light."

Through my loneliness and despair, God had encouraged and inspired me through Charlie's words. While I was still suffering from the dark days I had been experiencing for some time now, and still dealing with the lingering ache in my spine, I was desperately seeking to go from the darkness to the light. Indeed, dark does happen. It had happened to me, shadowing me from all that God had in store for my life. I didn't know what lie ahead in the Czech

Republic, but I knew I had to go. I felt God calling me to do so, for whatever purpose He needed me to fulfill.

Once our team arrived in the Czech Republic and, eventually, camp headquarters in Daňkovice, I began to question myself as to why I had joined the excursion. I was still in a mental and emotional funk, one that I so desperately wanted to work my way out of but didn't have the fortitude or the physical capacity to do so. I was in a place where I could serve God, my fellow man, and to better my own self.

I remained in the pit I had been in for months. I needed an epiphany, something that would help me to recall all that had been good in my life. I needed a diversion from the depressive emotions I had been experiencing for far too long. While I had been inspired by Charlie Marus's sermon, I continued struggling with depression and loneliness as we set out on Youth English Camp 2010.

One day during camp, we all gathered for what the Czech leadership team termed as "Christian Time". We did not have this special program allocated during the 2009 Youth English Camp. Basically, "Christian Time" was a voluntary meeting where anyone attending the camp could join with members of both our American team and the Czech leadership team in a period of reflecting on the Christian faith, prayer, music and an invitation to know Christ in a personal and intimate way. I only attended because I was the American team leader. Inwardly, I was still digging myself out of the deep black hole my mind, body, soul and spirit had been engulfed in for several months. Outwardly,

I would display a positive demeanor toward the mission at hand as we began the special session.

Evidently, and unbeknownst to me or, for that matter, anyone present, God had a special plan for that afternoon, one that would unfold during and after "Christian Time". While the session wasn't mandatory and other activities were scheduled for those wishing to not attend, every young person and adult leader was present.

As the discussion centered around the true meaning of a Christian life, the Holy Spirit began to move in the hearts of the young people. The room began to erupt in praise and adoration toward God, and unbelieving souls would give their hearts over to Jesus. It was the most spiritual place I had ever been in; that is, until I stepped outside for a moment.

As I exited the meeting room to go outdoors for some fresh air to breathe, I gazed over the gorgeous mountainside of Daňkovice. Into the far-off distance, I viewed a rain shower pouring over a remote mountain. Then suddenly, within only a matter of seconds, the rain stopped and the sun began to beam over the entirety of those same rolling mountains.

As I stood there, all alone, it was as if God stood next to me. There appeared over the mountain range the highest, clearest and most beautiful rainbow I had ever witnessed. The magnificent radiance and the mixture of vibrant colors was breathtaking, and I felt as if I was in the presence of the Heavenly Father.

60 CENTS

At that very moment, God spoke to my heart, telling me that I was going to be okay, and that I needed to hand all of my pain, worry and sorrows over to Him, and He would deliver me from the depression I had been struggling with for too long. Finally, I was experiencing the "light" Charlie had spoken about in his powerful message a few Sunday's ago.

With a heart filled with joy, I held my hands up toward Heaven and shouted my praises to God. The dark images that had penetrated my soul were replaced with images of light. I could clearly see the path that I needed to walk; one that would take me to places I never knew existed. I was a transformed man, nothing like I had ever been before. Instantaneously, my desire for my life was to turn away from any negativity that had entered into it, and to only do good and no harm in all that I did.

The remainder of the 2010 Youth English Camp was a celebration of the power of the Holy Spirit. It changed my life forever, giving me renewed purpose and zest for life. I was a new man, ready to cast aside many of my old ways. I felt whole again and comfortable in my own skin.

God had held my hand through my darkest time. It had only been a few months since I had given up hope for life. Now, it was time for me to live a renewed, resurrected life, in God's light.

There was so much I wanted to do now, and one of my top priorities was to research the murders, trial and executions involving my Granddaddy and Great-Granddaddy Hulsey.

It had been twenty-three years since that fateful day at the Goodyear Golf Course, when I encountered Lavay McCullough and then learned from Momma the truth of the family secret that had been kept from me for so long.

The time had now come for me to discover all of the sordid facts surrounding my family's heritage. I still remained upset and angry with Daddy for not telling me about what had taken place back in the early 1930s. I couldn't get over the fact that he had hidden all of this from me up until his death.

I would soon set out on a course to fulfill my desire to know more about my grandfathers, and to fill in all of the missing pieces regarding what occurred. Whether or not I would ever come to terms with Daddy's secrecy and my anger and frustration toward him seemed improbable.

The breathtaking mountains of Daňkovice, Czech Republic.

CHAPTER THIRTEEN: REVELATION

Returning back home from the Czech Republic and adjusting to a new-normal way of life was the start of a new beginning for me. I had experienced a few highs and many lows over the past eight months, and it was time to refocus on what was important in life – faith, family, career, service to my fellow man and community and, for me personally, researching the story of my grandfathers and all that took place eighty years prior. It would become a formidable undertaking of discovery as I sought to learn more about my Hulsey family heritage.

On one particular crisp fall afternoon, I had just completed an AFLAC enrollment with one of my clients, the City of Cedartown government employees. Cedartown is the county seat of Polk County, Georgia, approximately thirteen miles west of Rockmart.

The Polk County Courthouse is located in the heart of Cedartown. It was there, in a courtroom inside the same building that stands today, where my grandfathers were arraigned, indicted, tried, convicted and sentenced to death by electrocution for the murder of Cliff Jones, one of the three men they were purported to have cold-bloodedly and senselessly shot to death at the Hulsey farm on June 19, 1930.

Cedartown City Hall is situated only a few blocks from the county courthouse, in a city complex consisting of City

Hall, city police and fire departments, the Cedartown Theater and the Cedartown Public Library. After completing my AFLAC duties at city hall, I decided to walk over to the library. I was curious to see if, by chance, they may have some sort of historical information related to my grandfathers.

The librarian was not familiar with the story that had taken place so many years ago. She determined through library records that there was no written account of the incidents on file there. She suggested that I take time to browse through some of the old *Cedartown Standard* newspaper files that had been transferred to microfilm. I was amazed to see that there were editions of the newspaper available from the early 1900s. I felt as if I might be on to something as I loaded up the microfilm from 1930, 1931 and 1932.

Sure enough, as I rolled the film through the projector, news articles regarding my grandfathers and all that had taken place eight decades ago began to emerge before my startled eyes. Seeing for the first time the headline from the *Cedartown Standard* June 26, 1930 edition, *Triple Slaying Arouses Polk County Officers – Five Arrests Made in Brutal Rockmart Mystery Murder – Police Still Active in Their Search for Evidence That Will Solve Polk's Gruesome Slaying*, was a breathtaking experience.

As I continued on in my search, I would uncover several more articles detailing the brutal murders, the arrests of my grandfathers for murder and of three others as accessories to the murders, reports from the trial and accounts of several pleas and stays of execution rendered over a course of two-plus years after sentencing. It was all so fascinating and gave me pause to reflect on how well Momma was able to recall and share the story almost twenty-three years prior.

It also made me wonder how Daddy had kept this such a secret for so long. I kept asking myself, "How could Daddy have not told me all of this?" And to think that it all wasn't just locked inside Daddy's heart and mind, but that information surrounding the murders, the trial and executions had been available for my discovery for my entire life at a library close to home. I continued my research and made copies of each article from the Cedartown Standard that detailed any information regarding my grandfathers.

Days later, I returned to Cedartown on a personal reconnaissance mission to gain more information. I went to the Superior Court Clerk's office at the Polk County Courthouse seeking any records they might have. Through extensive research, I was able to unearth court dockets and transcripts from the arrest, arraignment and indictment phases of the legal process. Contained within the body of these documents were newspaper articles from *The Rockmart News*, a newspaper that would eventually become known as *The Rockmart Journal.*

I had been informed that transcripts from the actual trial had been damaged and/or destroyed in a fire that had occurred in the courthouse years ago. Years later, Johnny Pannell, a longtime friend and former city attorney for Rockmart during a portion of my time serving on the City

Council, uncovered the transcripts in an exhaustive search through court records. They had not, in fact, been destroyed. I would eventually gain access to and receive copies of the trial transcripts.

Surfing through various search engines on the Internet, I came across archival information from *The Atlanta Journal, The Atlanta Constitution,* and from the Associated Press. Articles found within the vaults of these publications and news resources, as well as from other publications from throughout the United States that also came to light through Internet searches revealed the fullness of the story that Momma had shared with me years ago.

The murders, trial and executions were big news back in the 1930s and made national headlines not just in Georgia, but across the country in various newspapers, including: *The Titusville Herald* out of Titusville, Pennsylvania; *The Bradford Era* from Bradford, Pennsylvania; *The Neosho Daily Democrat,* of Neosho, Missouri; *The San Antoni Light* from San Antonio, Texas; *The Anniston Star* from Anniston, Alabama; the *Modesto News-Herald,* out of Modesto, California; and, the *Montana Standard* from Butte, Montana, to name a few.

I was able to find online links that led me to finding the death certificates of Cliff Jones, Lige Harper and Ernest McCullough. Interestingly, the initial certificates show the cause of death for each of the three victims to be "gunshot to the head". The death certificates would later be amended by the attending physician, Dr. T.E. McBryde of Rockmart, to show the cause of death to simply be "murder". These were changed on July 22, 1930, only a few days after the guilty verdicts were handed down against my grandfathers.

Additionally, I obtained, through the Baldwin County, Georgia Probate Court death certificates of both Granddaddy and Great-Granddaddy Hulsey. On each of their documents, the cause of death is listed as "legal electrocution".

With the assistance of so many thoughtful and kind people, I had committed my resources of time, energy and finances toward discovering all I could about the family story Daddy had never offered one inkling of enlightenment about. It was mind-blowing knowing that all of this data had existed for so many years and had never once crossed my path. To me, it seemed downright shameful that it had been kept from me for such a long time, particularly by Daddy.

The following is a compendium of my findings through extensive research that expounds on the story Momma had shared with me back in August of 1987...

Staff Correspondent L.A. Farrell (1881-1945) reported the shocking murders and the subsequent arrests and inquisitions in the June 21, 1930 edition of *The Atlanta Constitution*:

The Atlanta Constitution June 21, 1930 "Five Bound Over In Triple Killing" Staff Correspondent L.A. Farrell
Used with permission of The Atlanta Journal-Constitution

BRAD HULSEY

ROCKMART, GA. June 20 – Five men charged with first degree murder tonight sit closed-mouthed in the county jail up at Cedartown while in this town's only morgue its three slabs hold three bullet-torn bodies as a result of what the police say started out to be the gentle trimming of two men who worked by two men who didn't – a poker picnic which became a massacre because the supposed "suckers" won all the money.

A coroner's jury this afternoon directed that the five men, William Hulsey and his two sons, Ray and Fred; Tom Hicks, his son-in-law, and L.E. McCullough be bound over to the grand jury on charges of murder for the slayings of Cliff Jones, Lige Harper and Ernest McCullough, whose bodies were found late yesterday pitched headlong in an abandoned well four miles east of here.

Solicitor General S.W. Ragsdale, of the Tallapoosa Circuit, who came here from Cedartown to co-operate with Judge W.B. Leonard, the coroner, in conducting the inquest, said the five men would be held without bond until the case is taken before the grand jury early in August.

Though only Hicks has made any statement, the others refusing to talk, and Hicks only giving, according to Colonel Ragsdale, a piece-meal version of what he knows of the triple-shooting, the solicitor general tonight said he believed the prosecution, aided by Chief of Police Paul Smith, of Rockmart, and Deputy Sheriff A.G. Chandler, "had forged the strongest chain of circumstantial evidence ever assembled in this circuit," adding that he would demand the death penalty for all five of the accused when they are brought to trial.

60 CENTS

This circumstantial evidence, together with the testimony of almost a score of witnesses was presented to Judge Leonard's jury this afternoon at an inquest for which Rockmart practically declared a holiday and more than a thousand people sought to attend and resulted in the binding over of the five men to the grand jury.

The story of the gruesome killing and what the authorities believe led up to it is perhaps best told by Chief Smith who summed up his own and his sides' investigation in making his report to Solicitor General Ragsdale.

"As far as we can learn," Chief Smith said, "The Hulseys, William and his son, Fred, sought to engage Jones, Ernest McCullough and Harper in a poker game. The Hulseys were known to be gamblers. They live several miles east of town and have been arrested numerous times for gaming and on other minor charges.

"The three men, McCullough, Jones and Harper work at night and therefore were free in the day time. Early Wednesday they met L.E. McCullough, who is not related to Ernest McCullough. All of them went out to the Hulsey place about noon and began drinking home-brew, later starting to play poker.

"The game was played out in the open, about 150 yards from the Hulsey house where they spread out some newspapers on the ground beneath small shade trees. That they had considerable to drink during the game is evidenced by the fact that almost a score of empty beer bottles were found at the scene of the slayings and some bottles of home-

brew which had not been opened. In a smokehouse not far away we also found about 20 bottles of beer on ice.

"According to L.E. McCullough, the only living person who has talked of the game, only the two Hulseys and Ernest McCullough and Jones were in the poker game. It is our theory that Jones and Ernest McCullough had a little money when the game started but that the Hulseys had something like $150 between them.

"L.E. McCullough says he left the Hulsey place after taking a few drinks and watching the game get started. He declares that when he got back home he missed his pocket-knife and returned to the Hulsey place, where he says he thought he left it. During the time he was absent, he says, Ernest McCullough and Jones appear to have won consistently, for he says that he when he returned Ernest McCullough had more than $100 in his stack, while Jones had about $25 or $30.

"L.E. McCullough says that he remained around the scene about five or ten minutes hunting his knife and during that time there was a constant wrangle, all of the four players showing signs of having done considerable drinking. Harper, he says, was not there when he made his second visit, but that on his second homeward trip he passed Harper walking toward town.

"At the inquest today J.W. Bramlett and his son, who live near the Hulsey place, testified that about four o'clock yesterday afternoon they heard two pistol shots about 30 seconds apart and a third shot about 10 minutes later.

SHOT THROUGH HEAD

"All three men were shot through the head from the rear, each bullet passing completely through the head of the victim and scampering over the open country. None of them have been found. Ernest McCullough was shot through the left side of his head and Jones through the right side. The bullet which pierced Harper's head entered at about the center.

"From these finding and the report of Dr. T.E. McBride we have theorized that the two poker players were shot dead as they were seated about the game, the killer standing between them and shooting once to the right and once to the left, and that Harper, when he returned from town, was shot and killed after he had discovered that his two companions were slain."

Chief Smith testified as to his findings at the inquest. Dr. McBride and the two Bramletts also told of hearing the three shots.

L.E. McCullough, testifying at the inquest, where he was examined by Colonel Ragsdale, declared that he did not remain at the Hulsey place but about 30 minutes and about 10 minutes on his second. He declared that he did not see or know anything of the killings until he heard it on the streets in Rockmart Thursday night.

What the solicitor general said was one of the strongest links in the prosecutor's chain of evidence is the finding of the wagon which the police believe was used to carry the three bodies from the scene of the crime to the abandoned and dry well, about a mile and a half from the Hulsey home.

The wagon was found this morning in the Hulsey barn. This phase of the investigation was handled by D.C. Sparks, Rockmart detective.

PATHWAY SELDOM USED

"The pathway from the highway to the well is seldom used," *Sparks said, testifying at the inquest. "I examined the wagon tracks found on it and discovered that three of the wheels of the wagon which passed over it were of normal size, but the fourth, the left front, appeared to be heavier and about two inches wider than regular wheels, one that is on a cultivator or some other heavy farm instrument.*

"Today, when I went to the Hulsey place I found a wagon in the barn. The wheels measured exactly the same as the imprints on the pathway. There was blood on the tongue and about the sides. Its bed was missing but it appeared to have recently been torn out."

Just what part Ray Hulsey and Hicks played in the killing, if any, both Chief Smith and Solicitor General Ragsdale said they were not certain.

Ernest Watts, an employee of the railroad, who worked about a half a mile from the Hulsey home on Wednesday afternoon, testified that he met Ray Hulsey about 5 o'clock that day headed for the Hulsey home and carrying a can of gasoline, which the police later found a few yards from the house in a thicket.

J.G. Weaver, who operates an auto livery in Rockmart, testified that Ray Hulsey came to his place of business early Thursday morning and rented a car, telling him that "he had to get his wife out of town."

"I rented him the car which he was supposed to bring back within a couple of hours," Weaver declared. He didn't come back and yesterday morning I went out to his place and got it."

HICKS FEARED HULSEY

Concerning young Hicks, F.E. Bishop testified that Hicks came barefooted to his home sometime between midnight and daybreak Thursday morning and told him that he feared Fred Hulsey and wanted to stay there.

"Hicks stayed at my place the remainder of the night," Mr. Bishop testified. He told me that he had fled from his own home which is just across the road from Ray Hulsey's because he said he had met Fred Hulsey there and Fred had told him that 'he needn't run.' He said Fred told him that he had already killed three men and hidden them away and could do the same with him."

The solicitor general halted the inquiry to tell the jury that Hicks had made similar statements to him during interview with the prisoner in the Polk County jail early this morning.

Deputy Sheriff Chandler also proved a strong witness against young Hicks when he showed the jury a bloodstained shirt which he said he found earlier in the day during a visit to Hicks' house.

The jury deliberated almost an hour before returning its verdict and brought such surprise when all five were accused.

William and Fred Hulsey and L.E. McCullough, who until the time of the inquest had been held here were immediately shackled together and taken under heavy guard to Cedartown where they were placed in cells alongside of Hicks and Ray Hulsey, who had been taken there last night.

Solicitor General Ragsdale and Chief Smith also went to Cedartown, where they said they would remain "until every angle of this awful case has been cleared up to the satisfaction of the public."

Staff reports from the Cedartown Standard expounded on portions of Farrell's story –

Cedartown Standard June 26, 1930 "Triple Slaying Arouses Polk County Officers: Five Arrests Made In Brutal Rockmart Mystery Murder"
Used with permission of Otis Brumby III, Publisher, Times-Journal, Inc.

Polk County experienced the most gruesome slaying of its history last Thursday. Three men, Cliff Jones, Lige Harper and Ernest McCullough are dead. The badly mutilated bodies of the three men were found in an abandoned well, three miles southeast of Rockmart off the Dallas and Atlanta Highway.

60 CENTS

Chance Discovery
The bodies were discovered by Alonso Sorrells, who accompanied by his son were searching for bees in that vicinity. Their curiosity was aroused by the finding of a man's shoe and the fresh imprints of what appeared to be a horse drown (sic) wagon. Following the trail, they came to the abandoned well which revealed the victim's bodies.

Coroner Leonard and Deputy Sheriff Chandler were called to the scene and after assisting in extricating the bodies ordered them removed to the Cochran undertaking parlors in Rockmart. Although the three men were not known to Rockmart authorities, they were identified by employees of the Goodyear Mills where two of the three men had been employed.

Police Act Quickly
Prompt action by the county police authorities, who made good use of a number of clues in the mystery case resulted in the arrest of five men – four principals and one material witness. Bill Hulsey and his two sons, Fred and Ray and Tom Hicks are held as principals on suspicion. A man named Luddie McCullough, who is no relation to one of the victims by the same name, is held as a material witness. All five men are confined in the local jail.

Police authorities say they had learned that McCullough drove the three Hulseys, Hicks and the three victims – Cliff Jones, Lige Harper and Ernest McCullough, in a wagon to a clearing in the woods near Hulsey's home.

There they played poker, officers said. They said they found blood spots in the clearing where the men had allegedly had the poker game Wednesday. The condition of the bodies indicated that the men were slain Wednesday, Coroner Leonard said.

Evidence Found
The running gear of Bill Hulsey's wagon bore blood stains, and its body had been burned, police announced. Mule prints of an animal that was unshod on his rear feet were found near the well, and police said Hulsey's mule had no shoes on his hind feet. Gray mule hair was also discovered near the well. Hulsey's mule is gray.

Maintain Innocence
All of the men held in the case have refrained from making any statements relative to the killing other than to maintain their utter innocence of any implication in the slaying.

Solicitor Ragsdale, who has been tireless in his efforts to solve the gruesome crime in the county and states behalf, said that he had procured other important evidence that would aid considerably in the prosecution of the case, but he was withholding the information at this time.

It is rumored that further evidence in the case may be expected at any time. All of Polk County law enforcement officials are determined that every effort will be expended to apprehend and convict the guilty in this most horrible crime.

Court transcripts show that the February 1930 term of the Grand Jury of Polk County Superior Court had been adjourned. The next term of the Grand Jury was scheduled to convene in August 1930. Solicitor General Ragsdale was eager to move on with the case against my grandfathers and the other three men. Ragsdale was able to convince Judge Price Edwards that the February 1930 Grand Jury should immediately be reconvened in special session on Friday, July 11, 1930, for indictment of Granddaddy and Great-Granddaddy Hulsey in the murders of the three men. The story was reported by the *Associated Press* and printed in *The Atlanta Constitution:*

The Atlanta Constitution July 14, 1930 "Hulseys Face Trial In Triple Murder"
"Father and Son To Answer Charges at Cedartown Today"
Used with permission of The Associated Press Copyright© 2016. All rights reserved

CEDARTOWN, Ga. July 13 – (AP) Solicitor General S.W. Ragsdale of the Tallapoosa Circuit announced here today that William Hulsey and his son, Fred, will go on trial at a special term of court here tomorrow charged with the murder of three young men whose mutilated bodies were found in an abandoned well near Rockmart June 20.

They were indicted Friday at a special term of the grand jury. The grand jury will meet again tomorrow to consider the cases of William Hulsey's other son, Ray, his son-in-law, Tom Hicks, and L.E. McCullough, who have been held in jail with the others since the inquest over the three bodies.

The men slain were Cliff Jones, Lige Harper and Ernest McCullough, who was not related to L.E. McCullough.

Ragsdale said he did not expect the grand jury to charge Ray Hulsey, Hicks and L.E. McCullough with anything more serious than being accessories to the slaying.

Testimony was introduced at the inquest that show that William and Fred Hulsey, said by police to be professional gamblers, invited the three men to their home on June 18 for a drinking and gambling party. The money, however, was won by the visitors. No testimony to the actual slaying was adduced but officers said their investigation showed Ernest McCullough and Jones probably were shot to death as they sat on the ground playing. They said they believed Harper was slain when he came back to the place after a trip to town, and learned that his companions had been killed.

Officers said they had found blood stains on a wagon at the Hulsey place, that the bed of the wagon had recently been destroyed, and that the wagon's wheels fit tracks leading to the well in which the bodies were found.

Witnesses at the inquest also quoted Hicks as saying Fred Hulsey told him he had "already killed three men."

At the time of the inquest officers said they were not quite clear as to the connection of Ray Hulsey, Hicks and L.E. McCullough with the slaying, if there were any connection.

As illustrated in the Associated Press's account, Solicitor General Ragsdale believed he had enough evidence, albeit it circumstantial, to begin the trial of the State vs. William Hulsey, alias Bill Hulsey, and Fred Hulsey, only twenty-five days after the murders of the Cliff Jones, Lige Harper and

Ernest McCullough. Hardly enough time for my grandfathers and their attorney, William G. McRae to prepare and mount a defense against the charges.

It is not for me to determine if they were given ample time to prepare, and I am certainly not insinuating that my grandfathers were innocent of the charges they were facing. The fact remains that they were tried, convicted and executed for the murder of Cliff Jones. It only seems appropriate, however, that the court could and should have waited until the August 1930 Grand Jury was convened, thus providing the defense a more appropriate and sensible time frame for preparation prior to trial.

Court transcripts show that Defense Attorney McRae filed a motion for continuance until the regular August 1930 term of the court. McRae was appearing before the court on July 14, 1930, after having been hired by friends and relatives of my grandfathers only three days earlier on July 11, 1930, the same day the indictments were handed down.

McRae was unable to meet with my grandfathers on July 11th because they had already been transported from Cedartown back to the jail in Rome, Georgia, where they were incarcerated. McRae appears to have been handicapped by not having enough time to do his pre-trial groundwork. The transcripts from the Motion for Continuance reveal the following:

Defendants show that said indictment was found by the Grand Jury of Polk County on the 11th day of July, which is only three days ago. That after said indictment was found, friends and relatives of these defendants employed William G. McRae, of Atlanta, Georgia, an attorney at law, to represent these defendants on the trial of said indictment the same day they were returned, and that said attorney was unable to confer with these defendants due to their absence from the county until after 5 o'clock P.M. July 11, 1930.

That these defendants have been advised by their said attorney, William G. McRae, that said attorney has not been able to get ready to try said case because he has not had sufficient time since his employment to make a full investigation of the circumstances surrounding the homicide and to find witnesses who these defendants believe can and will testify to facts which will establish the innocence of these defendants.

The Motion for Continuance filed by McRae goes on to portray an urgency on the court's part to begin the trial while there is a sense of "excitement" throughout the county:

These defendants further show that there is prevalent in this county a degree of excitement against these defendants as a result of the extraordinary circumstances surrounding the killing of the deceased and Lige Harper and Ernest McCullough at the same time, which renders it unsafe for these defendants to go to trial at the term of this court. These defendants aver that the killing of these three persons aroused such extraordinary excitement in the minds of the people of this county that it influenced the calling of this special term of this court and the recalling of the February term grand jury within a few days after said homicides were committed for the sole main purpose of placing these defendants upon immediate trial before said excitement should have an opportunity to subside.

McRae goes on to argue in the Motion that, due to certain news articles that had been published in *The Rockmart News* soon after the murders had been committed, the unsafe environment placed upon the trial called for a continuance until the excitement could dissipate:

Defendants aver that a more atrocious crime was never committed in this county than the killing of these persons; that the fact that three men were killed and their bodies hidden in an abandoned well would have created such an extraordinary degree of public excitement is self-evident, and that such excitement should be against these defendants because of their association with the three deceased persons immediately preceding their death was a foregone conclusion in view of the attendant circumstances involving liquor, home-brew and gambling, the shooting of these men from the rear, and the use of one of these defendants' wagon in disposing of the bodies. Defendants offer as evidence of the extraordinary public excitement against them which makes it unsafe for them to go on trial at this term of court certain news items and editorials which were published and widely circulated throughout this county by The Rockmart News, Rockmart, Georgia, a weekly newspaper published near the scene of the homicides.

At this point in his Motion for Continuance, McRae pointed

to three specific articles that he believed would rouse excitement throughout the county and that, according to the transcript:

Contain matter unjustly harmful and prejudicial for these defendants, that they are villifying (sic) and untruthful and the inferences necessarily to be drawn from them and actually drawn from them by a large number of citizens of this county eligible for service upon a jury in this court would so tend to prejudice them against these defendants that it is unsafe for them to go upon their trial so soon after the commission of said homicides and the inflaming of the public mind against them by said news articles and editorials, and has made it almost impossible for them to secure a fair and impartial trial on this charge. Defendants aver that the principles of justice require a postponement of this trial to the August Term, 1930, of this court.

Included within the body of the Motion for Continuance were the three news articles from *The Rockmart News* McRae eluded to in his arguments. In viewing the actual newspaper clipping of the first article, it was dated the day of the murders, June 19, 1930.

Realistically, the reporting could not have occurred until at least one or two days after the murders had taken place. *The Rockmart News* was circulated weekly on Thursdays, so one can only speculate that, while the newspaper indicates a publish date of June 19, 1930, it was not placed into circulation until one or two days after. After reading the articles, one can draw their own conclusion as to the validity of McRae's claim that the articles are inflammatory and would cause my grandfathers to not receive a fair and impartial trial:

The Rockmart News June 19, 1930 "Three Mutilated Bodies Found In Well"
Used with permission of Otis Brumby III, Publisher, Times-Journal, Inc.

The most gruesome crime to have been committed in the history of Rockmart came to light Thursday afternoon when Alonzo Sorrells accompanied by his small son while searching for a bee tree, found a man's shoe and near by the track of a one horse wagon drawn by a small mule. Following this trail, it led to a deserted well on the old York place some six miles southeast of Rockmart. Going to the well Mr. Sorrells looked in and saw a man's foot. He hurriedly came to Rockmart and informed city and county officers who rushed to the scene and found three mutilated bodies instead of one. Coroner Leonard and deputy sheriff Chandler were summoned, but after viewing the scene left for Cedartown, and it was with much difficulty that undertaker Cochran could get instructions to prepare the bodies for burial.

The murdered men; Lige Harper and Ernest McCullough are reported as having been employed at the Goodyear Mill and Cliff Jones a workman at the New Way Dry Cleaning plant.

The bodies were badly mutilated and further examination revealed the fact that they had been shot.

Just before midnight officers Smith, Sparks and Hagan

assisted by Barrett and Raiford, arrested and jailed Will Hulsey and son Fred, also Tom Hicks. Others under arrest are Ray Hulsey and L.E. "Luddie" McCullough. The latter having acted as taxi driver who carried the three unfortunate men to a poker game Wednesday afternoon. He identified Will and Fred Hulsey as two of the men there. Each of the deceased men had families and carried insurance.

It is reported that the crime was committed at or near the home of Will Hulsey and from near there a paper containing blood, playing cards and some money has been brought in for evidence to be used in the coroner's trial Friday afternoon. Watch next week's issue for developments.

The Rockmart News June 26, 1930 "Five Under Arrest" Used with permission of Otis Brumby III, Publisher, Times-Journal, Inc.

The coroner's investigation of the triple slaying of Cliff Jones, Lige Harper and Ernest McCullough resulted in the imprisoning of Bill Hulsey and his two sons, Fred and Ray, Tom Hicks, a son in law, and Luddie McCullough is being held without bond as a material witness.

Hundreds visited the deserted well last Sunday.

Officers have quietly worked to knit together every thread of evidence possible. Solicitor Ragsdale, who will be assisted by Maj. Homer Watkins, the latter being retained by the relatives of the three murdered men, feels that the case is being unusually well developed, no stone is left unturned, and the demand for speedy justice will no doubt be carried out.

The prisoeers (sic) are being held for the August term of court.

The Rockmart News June 26, 1930 "Menace"
Used with permission of Otis Brumby III, Publisher, Times-Journal, Inc.

Rockmart has been awe stricken ever since last Thursday evening when the public was informed about the gruesome triple murder which occurred a few miles from here. That night the town was crowded with hundreds of people who stood upon the streets in large and small groups talking in solemn tones, and awaiting the arrival of the ambulance which brought the three bloody mutilated bodies to the undertaker.

There have been rumors of other brutal crimes committed in that "infected" area: of a man whisked to his death several years ago; of two other men who are now missing; of hold ups and robberies to infinity; of fights; of games where the unwary stranger was made to hand over the spoils should he happen to hold the winning cards; a death hunt for one of the gang who did not follow instructions; of mid-night rides with dead men; of people lured to this lanely (sic) place for various purposes; of bloody clothes being found; of mysterious forms that inhabit these mountain trails by night and wait for human life.

These and a thousand stories and truths can be heard on

the streets of Rockmart at any time of the day.

These crimes so repulsive and committed near our beautiful town have made us think of ghosts and booger men and goblins and we have a feeling akin to that which we had in childhood days when on Friday afternoons the smartest little girl or boy of our class rendered that awe inspiring recitation, "The Goblins Will Get You If You Don't Watch Out," and every little heart was filled with fear.

Some of these rumors are fiction and some are facts (sic), *but this is the conclusion of the whole matter: If such conditions existed or do exist; the public needs protection and demands it. And it is the duty of our County officers and every good citizen to rid this county of these human vultures who prey upon the public and are a menace to life.*

Defense Attorney McRae's Motion for Continuance was denied by Judge Price Edwards. While McRae and my grandfathers had only a couple of days to prepare their defense, an all-male jury of Polk County citizens was selected and seated from a pool of ninety-six men and the trial began on July 14, 1930 in the Superior Court of Polk County in Cedartown, Georgia, less than four weeks after the murders had taken place.

The Atlanta Constitution reported the beginning of the trial:

The Atlanta Constitution July 15, 1930 "HULSEYS ON TRIAL IN TRIPLE MURDER"
"Brother-in-Law Testifies Two Sought His Help in Disposing of Bodies"

60 CENTS

Used with permission of The Atlanta Journal-Constitution

CEDARTOWN, Ga. July 14 - Tom Hicks testified Monday in the trial of his father-in-law and brother-in-law, William and Fred Hulsey, that the defendants came to his home on the night of June 18, told him they had killed three men and asked him to help dispose of the bodies.

The Hulseys are charged with the murder of Cliff Jones, Lige Harper and Ernest McCullough, whose bodies were found June 20 in an abandoned well near Rockmart.

The state theory of the case is that the three men were killed by the Hulseys after they had been inveigled into a drinking and gambling party at the Hulseys' home and had won the Hulseys' money instead of being fleeced.

Ray Hulsey, another son of William Hulsey, denied from the stand that he had made a statement, attributed to him by officers, in which he was quoted as implicating his father and brother in the slaying.

Hicks said when the Hulseys came to his home with their proposal to help dispose of the bodies he demurred, saying he "didn't want to get into trouble," but they told him they already had taken the bodies five miles from their home, and that there was no danger. He said he made an excuse to get away, but came back later to find the Hulseys still there. He said he got away again on another excuse and spent the night at a neighbor's home in fear that he would be killed if he refused to fall in with their plans.

While the joint trial of father and son was in progress the grand jury still had under consideration charges against Ray Hulsey, Hicks and L. E. McCullough, who also have been held since the bodies were found. Officers have announced they would ask no more than an indictment charging the three with being accessories after the fact.

Judge Edwards, who called a special term of court for the trials, overruled two montions (sic) for continuance made by the defense. One motion was on the ground that Defense Attorney W. G. McRae, of Atlanta, had had insufficient time to prepare his defense. The other was on the contention that the jury had been improperly summoned.

Ninety-six talesmen were examined before the jury was completed and taking of evidence begun.

According to the transcripts of the trial obtained from the Polk County Superior Court Clerk's office, neither of my grandfathers testified in their own defense. Testimony from the trial centered around the circumstantial evidence that had been formed by the prosecution team in an attempt to prove that my grandfathers were the only logical killers of the three men. At no time during the coroner's inquest, the police investigation, or during the trial did anyone come forward to claim they had witnessed my grandfathers commit the murders, nor did anyone see them take the deceased bodies to the abandoned well and dump them into it. No murder weapon was ever produced.

The defense contended that L.E. "Luddie" McCullough, the

taxi driver who drove the three victims and my grandfathers to the Hulsey farm on the fateful day of the murders, was the actual killer. In his testimony, McCullough offered an alibi that showed, while he had in fact been at the card game on June 19, 1930, he had left and wasn't present when the murders took place.

As the trial ended, only after two days of testimony, *The Atlanta Constitution* offered this assessment of the day's proceedings:

The Atlanta Constitution July 16, 1930 "ARGUMENTS IN HULSEY TRIAL TO BEGIN TODAY"
"Both Sides Rest at Trial of Father and Son for Triple Slaying"
Used with permission of The Atlanta Journal-Constitution

CEDARTOWN, Ga., July 15 – (Special.) – With the taking of testimony concluded, both prosecution and defense at the trial of Bill and Fred Hulsey, charged with the murder of three men near Rockmart, rested with adjournment of court Tuesday night. Argument by counsel will begin at 9 o'clock Wednesday morning, with Solicitor S. W. Ragsdale and Homer Watkins speaking for the state and Defense Attorney W. G. McRae pleading on behalf of the defendants.

Outstanding development of the case Tuesday was the indictment by the grand jury of Ray Hulsey, son and brother of the defendants in the present trial, and of Tom Hicks as accessories to the murders.

Many witnesses were on the stand Tuesday, including Ray Hulsey, Mrs. Will Hulsey, L. E. McCullough, taxi driver who took the three victims to the scene of their deaths, relatives and friends of the deceased and others.

Both defense and state witnesses agreed on the incidents leading up to the killings, which occurred at a card game in a small patch of woods near the Hulsey home. The state's case contends that Fred Hulsey did the actual killing while his father, Bill Hulsey, helped dispose of the bodies by taking them in a wagon to an old well in the woods and throwing the bodies in.

The defense, while agreeing with the state case in so far as the preliminaries in the crime are concerned contends that McCullough, the taxi driver, did the actual killings. McCullough, however, testifying for the state, said that he was not present when the men were slain, having returned home for supper and other witnesses support this testimony.

Both of the defendants made no sworn statements from the stand this afternoon.

The case is expected to reach the jury sometime Wednesday afternoon with the probability of a verdict by night.

60 CENTS

Original and amended death certificate for Ernest McCullough.

CHAPTER FOURTEEN: RETRIBUTION

On Wednesday, July 16, 1930, after two days of testimony, the prosecution and defense presented their closing statements. Once completed, Judge Price Edwards charged the jury, who was then sent into the jury room to consider the guilt or innocence of my grandfathers.

After only four hours of deliberations, with little physical evidence to consider, and with only circumstantial evidence having been offered into testimony during the trial to go on, the jury returned a verdict of guilty against my grandfathers for the murder of Cliff Jones.

The verdict came with no request by the jury for mercy on my grandfathers' behalf. Judge Edwards set the sentencing for the next day, Thursday, July 17, 1930, at 9 a.m. It was a foregone conclusion that he would sentence them both to death in Georgia's electric chair.

Georgia, at that time, required a mandatory death sentence when there was a murder conviction without a request for consideration of mercy by the jury. *The Atlanta Constitution* offered this synopsis of the day's events:

The Atlanta Constitution – July 17, 1930 "FATHER AND SON DOOMED TO DIE IN CHAIR FOLLOWING CONVICTION IN TRIPLE MURDER"
"CEDARTOWN JURY FAILS TO DIRECT MERCY IN

VERDICT"
"William and Fred Hulsey Will Be First Father and Son to Be Executed in Georgia"
"JURY DELIBERATES ONLY FOUR HOURS"
"Defense, Claiming Lack of Time to Correctly Prepare Case, Plans Appeal"
Used with permission of The Atlanta Journal-Constitution

CEDARTOWN, Ga. July 16 – (Special) – Georgia's first father-son execution was in prospect tonight when a jury in superior court here found William Hulsey, and his son, Fred guilty of the murder of Cliff Jones, one of the three men slain in Rockmart's "poker massacre," returning a verdict without a recommendation for mercy, making a sentence of death in the electric chair mandatory.

The Hulseys are also under indictment for the murder of Lige Harper and Ernest McCullough, killed with Jones last month after a poker picnic on the Hulsey farm, four miles east of Rockmart, the state contending the Hulseys killed the three men after they had proved winners in the poker game.

Solicitor General S.W. Ragsdale, of the Tallapoosa circuit, who directed the prosecution, announced tonight that the Hulseys would be put on trial at the next term of court for the slaying of Harper and McCullough. Ray Hulsey, another son of William Hulsey, and Tom Hicks, the elder Hulsey's son-in-law are still held in jail here. They appeared as witnesses for the state.

L. E. McCullough, Rockmart taxi driver, who admits carrying the three men to the Hulsey farm, was released tonight. On the witness stand at their trial the Hulseys asserted that it was McCullough who fired the shots which killed the three men.

The conviction of the Hulseys came after the jury had deliberated four hours. The foreman, W. E. Zuker, declared that the 12 men who voted the verdict agreed not to make any public discussion of their deliberation, though he asserted that the verdict had been made almost an hour before it was returned to Superior Court Judge Price Edwards.

Judge Edwards announced that he would pass formal sentence and fix the date of execution at 9 o'clock tomorrow morning. Simultaneously, William G. McRae, of Atlanta, chief of defense counsel, announced he will file a motion for a new trial tomorrow and appeal to the supreme court in the event his motion is lost.

The murders of Jones, Ernest McCullough and Harper were considered the most brutal murders in this section. All three men had been shot in the back of the head, apparently as they had been seated around the poker game at the Hulsey farm. Their bodies were found a day after the murders, pitched headlong into an abandoned dry well two miles from where they were killed. Within a few hours after the discovery of the bodies the Hulseys were under arrest and charged with the crime.

Solicitor General Ragsdale is announcing that he would put the father and son to trial for the killings of Harper and

Ernest McCullough and said he planned to do so in order to forego any possibility of there "being a miscarriage of justice".

"I can see no reversible errors in the trial of this case," Colonel Ragsdale said. "But there is always the possibility that the supreme court may send it back because of some minor technicality. I think the death sentence against these two men will be obtainable in the other two cases and I am assuredly going to ask for it."

Colonel Ragsdale was assisted in the prosecution by Homer Watkins, of Atlanta, employed as a special assistant solicitor-general.

Attorney McRae, in announcing his plans, asserted the "Hulseys have only begun to fight."

"We did not have an opportunity to correctly prepare our defense," the lawyer said. "We were rushed to trial against our will. I think that in itself is grounds for a reversal."

The trial of the Hulseys was begun yesterday before Judge Edwards and has attracted large crowds to each session. The killing of the three men caused a sensation around Rockmart and many of the spectators who jammed Judge Edwards courtroom to hear the testimony were from that section of the county.

The following day, Judge Edwards handed down the mandatory death sentence to Granddaddy and Great-Granddaddy Hulsey. Newspaper accounts stated that

Great-Granddaddy had been worn down significantly by the events of the past four weeks. He appeared tired, depressed and lethargic. On the other hand, Granddaddy Hulsey was confident of his innocence and displayed no show of emotion as the sentence of death in the electric chair was passed.

Judge Edwards set the date of execution to be Wednesday, August 20, 1930, only sixty-two days after the murders occurred. The occasion was documented by *The Atlanta Constitution*:

The Atlanta Constitution July 18, 1930 "Hulsey Pleads With Judge For Time To Prepare To Die"
"Not Ready To Die, Says Convicted Slayer – Son Reiterates His Innocence"
Used with permission of The Atlanta Journal-Constitution

CEDARTOWN, Ga., July 17 – Pleading "I'm not ready to die," William Hulsey, convicted with his son for the slaying of one of three men the state charged were killed in a card game, stood before Judge Price Edwards to be sentenced Thursday morning and begged for as much time as possible to prepare himself before execution. The two were sentenced to die August 20.

The father collapsed in jail Wednesday night after a jury had returned a verdict of murder carrying the death penalty less than a month after the bodies of Cliff Jones, Lige Harper and Ernest McCullough were found in an abandoned well at

Rockmart, Ga. Physicians were summoned and stayed with him for several hours, according to county officials.

Fred Hulsey, the son, reiterated his innocence to Judge Edwards just before sentence was pronounced. "My father and I did not commit this awful crime," he said. "I believe we can prove that if given another trial."

Both received sentence with calmness but later the father had to be assisted back to his cell.

Defense attorneys immediately filed motion for a new trial. A date for hearing of the appeal is to be fixed Friday or Saturday.

Investigators charged that the three slain men were "taken for a ride" in a one-horse wagon because they won heavily in a card game in which they were expected to lose.

The prosecution during the trial described the Hulseys as professional gamblers and presented the theory that the men were shot in the back of the head while they were seated at a poker game on the Hulsey farm. Authorities said the slain trio were invited to the farm for a drinking and gambling party. Witnesses for the state testified the Hulseys borrowed a wagon to carry the bodies of the men to the well where they were found.

The defense based its contention that the trio were killed by L.E. McCullough, a taxi driver, who carried them to the Hulsey farm. McCullough, the taxi driver, and no relation to

Ernest McCullough, one of the slain trio, took to the stand as a state witness and said he took no part in the killing.

Ray Hulsey, brother of Fred and Tom Hicks, brother-in-law are under indictment as accessories after the fact.

With their executions having been set for August 20, 1930, my grandfathers were transported to the Floyd County Jail in Rome, Georgia to await their inevitable transfer to the Georgia State Prison in Milledgeville for their date with the electric chair. Their attorney, William G. McRae, would do as he said and mount an appeal for a new trial or, at the least, leniency. McRae's efforts would stall the executions for over two years.

On several occasions, Georgia Governor Richard B. Russell (who would eventually go on to be U.S. Senator from Georgia and would nominate Daddy to the U.S. Military Academy at West Point) would stay the executions to allow McRae more time to present any compelling new evidence. In a September 15, 1932 article from the *Cedartown Standard*, titled *"Hulseys Ask Governor for Stay,"* the appellate process and eventual outcome were detailed.

According to the article, the death sentences of my grandfathers were stayed by an appeal to the Georgia Supreme Court soon before the scheduled executions of August 20, 1930. The appeal was denied by the Supreme Court on Monday, July 6, 1931. On that same day, my grandfathers were re-sentenced to be executed on Friday, July 24, 1931.

Upon appeal by Defense Attorney McRae for the need of additional time to gather evidence that might exonerate my grandfathers, Governor Russell granted a sixty-day respite before the July 24, 1931 execution date. McRae could offer no additional compelling evidence for the death sentences to be overturned or for a new trial to be ordered. On Thursday, September 24, 1931, my grandfathers were once again re-sentenced to die in Georgia's electric chair, this time for Friday, October 9, 1931.

Granddaddy and Great-Granddaddy Hulsey were transported from Rome to Milledgeville for their date with the electric chair. Only a few hours before the executions were to occur, Governor Russell, after a plea from William G. McRae, granted yet another sixty-day respite. McRae then filed an extraordinary motion for a new trial, stating that there was not enough time for the defense to formulate an appropriate case before the trial and that he could possibly offer testimony that would refute many of the statements made during the trial.

On Friday, November 20, 1931, the Georgia Supreme Court passed an order superseding and staying the execution of sentence of death until such time that the motion for a new trial was heard and determined.

It would take several months for the Georgia Supreme Court to consider McRae's motion for a new trial. On Wednesday, August 24, 1932, after an exhaustive examination of the motion, the Supreme Court affirmed the action of the Polk County Superior Court. A new date of execution was then set for Friday, September 16, 1932.

On Thursday, September 15, 1932, only one day prior to the execution date, Governor Russell granted a thirty-day respite after McRae cited the fact that the Georgia State Prison Commission was not then in session. Additionally, McRae asserted that, while the Georgia Supreme Court had affirmed the action of the lower court, there were two justices who had favored clemency for my grandfathers.

The respite would last longer than thirty days as my grandfathers and their defense attorney would await a hearing before the State Prison Commission in their plea for commutation of the death sentences to a more lenient judgement. Appearing before the Prison Commission on Tuesday, November 1, 1932, William G. McRae presented the case for mercy and commutation of the sentence. After hearing the evidence, the Prison Commission refused to grant the plea for commutation and declined to interfere in the case further.

On Wednesday, November 2, 1932, my grandfathers were sent back to the Polk County Superior Court for re-sentencing. That day, they appeared before Judge J.H. Hutcheson, who set the new execution date for Friday, November 4, 1932. Granddaddy and Great-Granddaddy were taken back to Milledgeville to, once again, await their executions.

One day prior to the execution date, Defense Attorney McRae made one last-ditch plea to Governor Russell for commutation of the sentences. The governor would not intervene anymore. The final plea and setting of execution was reported in the *Cedartown Standard* one day prior to the sentences being carried out:

Cedartown Standard November 3, 1932 "Hulseys Face Execution On Friday"
Used with permission of Otis Brumby III, Publisher, Times-Journal, Inc.

Superior Court Judge J.H. Hutcheson in Cedartown ordered a new date of execution for November 4, 1932 after evidence was presented by the defense to the State Prison Commission on November 1, 1932. The Commission refused to grant the plea of commutation and declined to interfere in the case further.

A plea was delivered to Governor Russell on November 3, 1932 with an appeal for commutation of sentence. Governor Russell declines any further plea, thus allowing the sentences to be carried out the next day.

Having exhausted every means available in their fight for life, William Hulsey and Fred Hulsey will be executed at the State Prison in Milledgeville, GA on November 4, 1932.

I could find no evidence that there ever was an appeal to the Unites States Supreme Court. One would think that with over two years of appellate efforts having been made that, perhaps, William G. McRae would have looked to the highest court in the land for their consideration of clemency. Nevertheless, my grandfathers had nowhere else to turn. They would have to "face the music" and "meet their Maker," suffering their punishment for having been convicted of the murder of Cliff Jones.

I cannot comprehend how my grandfathers must have felt as they prepared for their executions. Obviously, Granddaddy Hulsey preferred to take his own life, instead of having to face the electric chair. I wonder if his suicide attempt was a result of shame, cowardice, or guilt. Maybe he was simply ready to get it all over with.

Momma's account to me of the execution day was nearly "spot on". All that she shared with me on that hot August day in 1987 bears true in an article written by the *Associated Press* that appeared in *The Atlanta Constitution* the day after the executions:

The Atlanta Constitution November 5, 1932 "Father And Son Go To Death Chair"
Used with permission of The Associated Press Copyright© 2016. All rights reserved

MILLEDGEVILLE, Ga., Nov. 4 – (AP) A father and son were electrocuted today for murder, the father protesting innocence and the son, after a suicide attempt, confessing sole guilt and pleading: "Don't kill my dad for something I did myself."

The dramatic confession of the son, 31-year old Fred Hulsey, came in the death cell after he had slashed his throat and left wrist with a safety razor blade. The suicide attempt came while the prison chaplain was reading Scriptures to Fred and his father, William, 58.

"I am the only one responsible," shouted Fred, hysterically. "My father only helped me to dispose of the bodies in order to help me out of my trouble." Guards prevented him from

further injuring himself.

The Hulseys were convicted of slaying Clifford Jones after a poker brawl on their farm near Rockmart, in north Georgia, in June, 1930, and were indicted, but not tried, for killing two other men.

Fred Hulsey admitted today that he slew Jones and Lige Harper and Ernest McCullough and said the father's only part in the crime was in helping him put the bodies in an abandoned well.

The suicide attempt – unexplained at the prison where razor blades are barred in the death cell – held up the execution for nearly four hours while prison authorities consulted Governor Richard B. Russell, Jr. The governor, in North Carolina for an address on behalf of the Democratic national ticket, was reached by telephone and ordered that the executions proceed if young Hulsey's wounds were not considered fatal.

Not long after the son, pale and nervous, his throat and wrist swathed in bandages, was led to the death chamber. His clothing bore the stains of his suicide attempt.

He sat down in the electric chair and addressed the small group of witnesses, consisting of prison attaches and newspapermen:

"I'll meet you all in heaven. I am glad I confessed this crime before I died."

Then he turned to the prison chaplain, Dr. E.C. Atkins and said:

"Please tell my father I'll meet him in heaven. I wish you would take the 60 cents in my pocket and send it to my little girl."

Physicians said that despite the razor wounds, his pulse was normal. The shock which killed young Hulsey was the shortest ever administered in Georgia – 15 seconds. The shock was applied at 1:48 p.m., eastern time. At 1:53 he was dead.

The body was removed. A big door clanged shut behind the father as he left the death cell for the short march to the execution chamber.

"The Lord is with me," he said simply, as he sat in the chair. "I am innocent of this crime, but I was there when it happened."

Jones, Harper and McCullough were found by relatives the day after they had been killed, each by a bullet in the head. Two of them had been shot in the back of the head. The relatives found the scene of the card game, with a number of empty beer bottles nearby. There were bloodstains near the scene of the game in the woods on the Hulsey farm. Tracks of a wagon and mule led the searchers to the well.

The death shock was applied to the father at 2:01. Four minutes later he was dead.

60 CENTS

Thus ended the first execution of father and son in Georgia.

The men were convicted on circumstantial evidence, but the state supreme court declared it was sufficient.

The principal witness for the state was L.E. McCullough, a taxi driver, who said he drove the three men who were slain and Fred Hulsey to the Hulsey place. The wagon tracks and a patch of mule hair on the ground where the mule drawing the wagon and its cargo had stumbled featured in the testimony. The Hulseys blamed L.E. McCullough (not related to the slain man) for the death, but McCullough established an alibi and testified for the state.

The executions had been scheduled for 10 a.m. after Governor Russell had spent most of yesterday examining records in the case. He refused to commute the sentences, however, and left late last night for a political rally in High Point, N.C.

Hulsey's suicide attempt today brought an order from Ike Hay, the governor's executive secretary, to hold up the executions until he had communicated with the governor and until the extent of Hulsey's wounds could be determined.

An uncle and an aunt of young Hulsey were in Milledgeville but did not witness the execution.

Prison officials said the bodies of the two men were claimed by Mrs. William Hulsey and were taken from here this afternoon by a Cartersville undertaking firm. The funeral services, it is understood, are to be in Aragon, near

BRAD HULSEY

Rockmart, probably on Sunday afternoon.

The suicide attempt was the first made by a prisoner in the death cell here awaiting the chair. The confession was the first publicly made by the son, naming himself as the slayer and his father as an accessory. Both pleaded not guilty at the trial. The father confirmed the son's confession.

It was fall of 2012. My research of the vile, secretive story that had been kept from me for twenty-five years by Daddy had come to a close. I had enough to corroborate what Momma had shared with me some twenty-three years prior regarding my grandfathers and their ultimate demise in Georgia's electric chair.

By learning much more than Momma had told me, and for the shameless, senseless actions of my grandfathers, I would be burdened with a load of guilt. They had taken the lives of three men. Each one of them had a wife and children. I could only imagine the struggles the families endured after the death of their husband and father, just like Maw Maw Vert, Daddy and Aunt Hope did.

There still remained unanswered questions that I continually pondered. Most of them couldn't be resolved, either because the individuals who had the answers were no longer living, or the persons who still lived and could provide clarity to the story would remained close-mouthed, just as Daddy did. If he had only told me about my grandfathers then, perhaps, my mind would be clear. For some unknown reason to me, Daddy was set on being taciturn, and it created so many questions in my mind.

60 CENTS

What was Daddy's life like after the executions of his father and grandfather? How was Maw Maw Vert able to cope with losing her husband and then raising Aunt Hope and him? Why did they remain in Rockmart? How heavy of a burden was it for him to bare his father's name? Do you think anyone else was partially or totally responsible for the three murders? Do you think Granddaddy's confession was true, or do you think he was taking the blame for Great-Granddaddy? Do you believe Granddaddy and Great-Granddaddy Hulsey received a fair and impartial trial? How did Granddaddy get the razor blade? Did you see Granddaddy while he was in prison? The answers to these and many other queries of mine will remain veiled from me for the rest of my earthly life.

There were other lingering questions that I mulled over frequently. Years after our chance encounter at the Goodyear Golf Course in Rockmart, was Lavay McCullough still alive? And, if so, would he be willing to talk about what he knew about his father's murder, and what life was like for him after his father's death?

Momma was suffering from Alzheimer's Disease and could no longer communicate with me. Phil, like me, knew nothing other than what I had been able to uncover. I was clueless on where and how to find Lavay McCullough or who, if anyone, could help get me in contact with him.

Soon, another chance encounter would change all of that.

CERTIFICATE OF DEATH
GEORGIA DEPARTMENT OF PUBLIC HEALTH
Bureau of Vital Statistics

#1897

Registered No.

WRITE PLAINLY WITH UNFADING INK—THIS IS A PERMANENT RECORD. Every item of information should be carefully stated in plain terms, so that it may be properly classified. Exact statement of occupation is very important. Was disease or injury caused by dangerous or insanitary conditions or occupation? Where was disease contracted if not at place of death?

1. PLACE OF DEATH

County _Baldwin_ Militia District (Number and Name) _319ce_ State of Georgia

City or Town _Milledgeville_ Length of residence in this city or town Yrs. Mos. Ds. _3_ NON-RESIDENT (Yes or No)

Street and Number (No.) _(Street)_ _Ga State Prison Farm_ Ward
(If death occurred in a hospital, give its name instead of street and number)

2. FULL NAME _Fred Hulsey_

Residence (City or Town) _State Farm Ga_ _(Street and Number)_ _(State)_

PERSONAL AND STATISTICAL PARTICULARS

3. SEX _male_
4. COLOR or RACE _white_
5. Single, Married, Widowed, Divorced (write the word) _married_

6. DATE OF BIRTH (month, day, year) _July 16ce 1901_

7. AGE Years _31_ Months Days If less than one day Hours Minutes

8. OCCUPATION
(a) Trade, profession or particular kind of work done, as spinner, sawyer, bookkeeper, etc. _Prisoner_
(b) Industry or business in which work was done, as cotton mill, sawmill, bank, etc. _State Prison_
(c) Date deceased last worked at this occupation (month and year)
(d) Total years spent in this occupation

9. BIRTHPLACE (P. O. Address) _Ga_

FATHER
10. NAME _William Hulsey_
11. BIRTHPLACE (P. O. Address) _Ga_

MOTHER
12. MAIDEN NAME _Cora Hulsey_
13. BIRTHPLACE (P. O. Address) _Ga_

14. INFORMANT (Signed) _W. L. Proctor_
(Address) _Warden State Prison farm_

19. BURIAL PLACE (Cemetery) _Wagon Cemetery_
(Postoffice) _Aragon Ga_ Date

20. UNDERTAKER (Signed) _Emmons-Long-Owen Co._
(Address) _Cartersville Ga._

MEDICAL CERTIFICATE OF DEATH

16. DATE OF DEATH _Nov - 4ce_ 19 _32_ at _1:40_ P.M.
(Month, Day, Year) (Hour)

17. I HEREBY CERTIFY, That I attended the deceased from _Nov - 4ce_ 1932 to _Nov - 4ce_ 1932

I last saw h__ alive on _Nov 4ce_ 1932 death is said to have occurred on the date and hour stated above. The principal cause of death and related causes of importance in the order of onset and duration of each:

Legal electrocution

Other contributory causes of importance:

What test confirmed diagnosis? (Specify whether autopsy, operation, laboratory, or clinical)

If death was due to external causes (violence) fill in also the following:

Was injury an accident, suicide, or homicide?

Where did injury occur (Specify city or town, if outside of limits, the county, and also the state)

Did injury occur in a home, public place or industry?

Manner of injury

Nature of injury

(Signed) _D. C. Woodson_ M.D.
(Address) _Milledgeville Ga._

18. FILED _Nov 5ce_ 1932
(Signed) _P. M. Watson_
(Local Registrar)

THIS IS TO CERTIFY THAT THIS IS A TRUE REPRODUCTION OF THE ORIGINAL RECORD ON FILE WITH THE STATE OFFICE OF VITAL RECORDS, GEORGIA DEPARTMENT OF COMMUNITY HEALTH. THIS CERTIFIED COPY IS ISSUED UNDER THE AUTHORITY OF CHAPTER 31-10, CODE OF GEORGIA, AND 290-1-3 DPH RULES AND REGULATIONS.

Deborah O. Aderhold

STATE REGISTRAR AND CUSTODIAN
GEORGIA STATE OFFICE OF VITAL RECORDS

County Custodian:
Issued by:
Date Issued: _November 14, 2011_

Any reproduction of this document is prohibited by statute. Do not accept unless embossed with a raised seal.

VOID IF ALTERED OR COPIED

Granddaddy Hulsey's death certificate

60 CENTS

CERTIFICATE OF DEATH
GEORGIA DEPARTMENT OF PUBLIC HEALTH
Bureau of Vital Statistics

#1898

Registered No.

Great-Granddaddy Hulsey's death certificate

240 | P a g e

CHAPTER FIFTEEN: REDEMPTION

By 2013, I had become very adept at "surfing" the Internet, primarily due to my years of extensive online research of my grandfathers through news sources and other historical websites. I had become a fan and frequent user of the popular social media website, Facebook. Through it, Facebook allowed me to keep informed on the comings and goings of so many of my family and friends.

I particularly enjoyed reconnecting with several of my Rockmart High School classmates and other current or former residents of our lovely hometown. Another huge benefit for me was my ability to stay in contact with my "other family" in the Czech Republic.

On one particular day in February 2013, I was scrolling through Facebook, reading posts and looking at photos of days gone by that had been posted by fellow "Rockmartians". I heard a "ding" sound reverberate over my computer speakers and noticed that I had received a message from someone. When I opened up the message box, the name "Andy McCullough" appeared. I had no clue who this was.

Occasionally, I would obtain requests from strangers to be their "friend" on Facebook that I would ignore. You never know who or what may be lurking through cyberspace with bad intentions of stealing your personal information or spreading a virus into your computer. I didn't know if that could happen via Facebook, but I usually didn't like taking that chance.

While I didn't know Andy McCullough, naturally his last name intrigued me. Against my usual practice and better judgement, I opened and began to read the message. I don't exactly recall the specific words that were included, but the gist of it was this:

"Hi, Brad. My name is Andy McCullough. I am from Boulder, Colorado. I believe you know my father, Lavay McCullough. He said that he met you several years ago. I am coming to visit my dad in April for a few days. On one Saturday while I'm in Georgia, Dad, my sister and her family and I are going to visit our aunt in Rome, Georgia. Dad would like to see you, so we were wondering if you could meet us somewhere in Rockmart that day before we travel on to Rome?"

I shook my head back and forth rapidly and blinked my eyes excessively just to make sure I was conscious and was truly seeing what I had just read. I read the message silently again, and then aloud to be certain that my ears were hearing what my eyes were reading. I slumped back in my chair and began grinning from ear to ear. "Lavay McCullough has a son," I thought to myself. "And he wants to bring him to see me. Lavay wants to see me!" I couldn't believe it.

For years, I clung to the hope that, one day, I would have the good fortune of meeting this kind man one more time.

I didn't know why Lavay wanted to meet with me, but it was obvious, at least to me, that he had a need or desire to do so. I gathered myself and then replied back to Andy with words of joy and an answer to his request, "Yes, Andy. It would be an honor for me to meet with your dad, you and your family."

Several days later, Andy sent me another Facebook message. In it, he asked if I could meet all of them in Rockmart on a particular Saturday afternoon at Sidekicks, a locally owned and operated restaurant. My schedule was clear, and I gladly accepted the invitation.

On the morning of our scheduled luncheon, I began wondering what the purpose of our meeting was to be. I knew I had several questions to ask of the McCullough family, particularly Lavay. In my own selfish manner, I deduced that the McCulloughs must have some specific need to see me, and that our rendezvous was somehow meant to be beneficial for them. I would soon learn that there was a greater and more personal meaning for our gathering, and that I would be the actual beneficiary.

On that muggy April Saturday afternoon in 2013, after my drive from our home in Powder Springs, I arrived at the restaurant. Pulling into the parking lot and turning off the ignition of my Honda CR-V, I viewed a line of humanity, and at the front of it was Lavay McCullough. I was happy to see him after nearly twenty-six years from our previous encounter at the Goodyear Golf Course.

In one hand, Lavay held a cane, probably to help with his

mobility due to the effect of his childhood polio, I presumed. I nervously smiled and waved as I exited my vehicle. For a moment, I thought to myself, "Here I am, the only Hulsey around, about to hold a meeting with a bunch of McCulloughs. What have I gotten myself into?"

After greeting Lavay, he introduced me to Andy. As a Baptist pastor and a doting father, Lavay was particularly proud to point out that Andy was serving as Missions Pastor at a church near Andy's family home in Boulder, Colorado. Given my prior service through mission trips in the Czech Republic, I felt an instant connection to Andy. Lavay then introduced his daughter, Laura Berrios and her husband, Jose, along with their children. The Berrios family resided in Georgia, where Laura is a writer.

Among her body of work, Laura writes articles for *The Atlanta Journal-Constitution* newspaper. Having been a sportswriter in a previous life, I felt a connection to Laura, as well. Not knowing the circumstances, I inquired about the whereabouts of Lavay's wife. Andy informed me that his mother, Gladys, had passed away in 2008. I expressed my sorrow to the family for their loss.

After being escorted to a table large enough to accommodate all of us, I took my seat next to Lavay. As I browsed through the menu it was difficult for me to think about eating. I wanted to know why Lavay wanted to meet with me after all of these years. I was prepared and willing to provide answers to any questions he and his family may have of me regarding the details I had discovered about the murders, trial, executions and aftermath involving both our family members.

All the while, as I looked at each one of them, I felt remorseful over the loss of their father and grandfather, Ernest McCullough, at the hands of Granddaddy and Great-Granddaddy Hulsey. I cannot recall what I ordered from the menu that day, but I do remember my inability to eat due to the overwhelming anxiety I was experiencing.

After each one of us placed our orders with the waitress, I began to chatter about the research I had been performing. I had brought with me two notebooks replete with newspaper articles, photos, copies of death certificates and other historical documents that pertained to the murders, trial and executions.

Andy, Laura and Jose gazed amazingly at the information I had obtained. Their faces revealed a curiosity to know more. I obliged by offering stories of what I had learned and in answering questions they asked of me to the best of my knowledge and ability.

Andy shared a photo they had brought along with them. It was the only photo Lavay had of his father. Looking upon it, my mind wandered back to 1930. I thought of how Ernest McCullough was such a young man, senselessly taken from his family by a gunshot to the back of his head, by my grandfathers, during a drunken poker game. The guilt I felt at that moment was overwhelming.

While there was an understandable desire on Andy's, Laura's and Jose's behalf to learn more, Lavay was a different story. He briefly glanced upon the volumes of materials I had garnered through my research, and he did look closely at photos I had of my grandfathers. There just seemed to be something else on his mind.

Lavay began asking me about Momma, how she was doing and where she was living. He asked about Aunt Dossie and told me he had heard about Uncle Willie's death in 2009. He recalled knowing Momma's only brother and my uncle, Lum Holland, and what a character he was.

Lavay spoke briefly of how, after his father's death and at the age of one-year-old his mother had sent him to live with his grandmother in Porterdale, Georgia. He said it wasn't easy living away from his mother, dealing with the aftermath of his polio, and not having a father to raise and teach him.

At this juncture, with my guilt for the sins of my grandfathers overflowing inside me, I offered an apology to Lavay and the entire family on my family's behalf. I thought to myself, "The McCullough family doesn't owe the Hulsey family forgiveness, but we certainly owe them reparation for the injustice of my grandfathers' transgressions."

Displaying honesty and humility in speaking about his father, and with tears welling up in his eyes, Lavay opened his heart to me. "Brad, I know you think your grandfathers were bad men. My father was a professional gambler just like them. People have told me how he shuffled cards like nobody else. He loved to drink. Yeah, my father had his issues, too."

Hearing this, I had to pause for a deep breath and fight back my own tears. I thanked Lavay for sharing that story with me. The message his words spoke to me was that, even though my grandfathers had murdered his father, that didn't necessarily make them the only "bad guys" that were present on that fateful day of June 19, 1930.

Our food soon arrived at the table. I looked down with a blank stare upon my lunch, wondering how I could possibly eat. As any good Baptist preacher would do, Lavay offered to say a blessing over the food. As we humbled ourselves before God by bowing our heads, he prayed a prayer that pierced the core of my heart in such a powerful and meaningful way.

Lavay's prayer, offered up to God, permeated my soul. I felt as if the Holy Spirit was speaking through Lavay. After giving thanks for the food and asking God's blessings over it, Lavay asked God's blessings upon me, my family, and upon Momma as she dealt with her physical and cognitive conditions. And then, through Lavay's prayer, God revealed to me the real reason I had been summoned by the McCullough family to meet with them.

"Lord, we ask today that if Brad is experiencing any guilt or frustration, that you would pour out your Holy Spirit upon him to comfort him and free him from these feelings. Let him know that all is forgiven. In Jesus name I pray. Amen!"

All along, and unbeknownst to me, our gathering that day had not just been for the McCullough's benefit. Indeed, it was for me, as well. The burden I had experienced for so many years over the murder of Ernest McCullough by my grandfathers was lifted right then and there.

I can never forget the dreadful deeds wrought by Granddaddy and Great-Granddaddy Hulsey, and I know that the Jones and Harper families suffered the loss of a loved one, as well. But through Lavay's redeeming prayer, a load was released that had a hold on me since 1987. At last, I could experience peace and a sense of closure regarding my grandfathers' ruinous actions.

As we departed the restaurant and said our goodbyes, I got into my car and paused to offer a prayer of thanksgiving to God and to ask His blessings upon the McCullough family. With it only being a mile away, I drove immediately to Aunt Dossie's house to tell her about our meeting.

Aunt Dossie was so glad to see me and hear that all had gone well. She shared her delight for Lavay McCullough's prayer of redemption. She proclaimed how good it was that I had learned about my Hulsey family heritage and that, with the time I had just spent with Lavay McCullough and his family, I could put aside my feelings of guilt and frustration that I had harbored for so many years.

Leaving Aunt Dossie's, I headed back toward home with comfort and confidence in the knowledge that the McCullough family had forgiven my family for the murders of Ernest McCullough. But something didn't seem right. I should have been experiencing tranquility in my heart but, instead, there still remained a sense of frustration and uneasiness within me.

While I had come to terms with my grandfathers' crimes, I still hadn't dealt with the fact that Daddy had kept the secret hidden deep inside from me for over twenty-five years. How could I ever forgive him for not telling me? Redemption came from God through Lavay McCullough, but peace would not be with me yet. I remained angry and frustrated with Daddy.

A meaningful time of fellowship with, from l to r: Laura Berrios, Lavay McCullough, me, Andy McCullough

CHAPTER SIXTEEN: RECONCILIATION

Having the opportunity to spend time with Lavay McCullough was a blessing. My heart was warmed by his redemptive grace, and by his family's welcoming and calming disposition as I spent that Saturday afternoon with them in Rockmart. I experienced forgiveness for the cruel deeds my grandfathers had committed against their father and grandfather, Ernest McCullough.

While it was a very meaningful and moving experience, I still felt empty inside due to my ongoing indignation toward Daddy. It was impossible for me to experience full and complete redemption while, lingering all around me, were the feelings of bitterness and contempt toward my deceased father. My spirit remained conflicted as I struggled with Daddy's purposeful cover-up of my grandfathers' transgressions and ultimate downfall.

It was only a matter of months after my afternoon with the McCulloughs that Kelly and I separated and eventually finalized our divorce. Aside from the end of a twenty-three-year marriage, it was a very trying time for our children. The anxiety and guilt I felt toward the kids for having their home shattered was overwhelming.

To add to my misery, the negative stress from a new positon I had taken a few months prior was taking a toll on me. Having suspended my active role with AFLAC, I was now the City Manager of Powder Springs. Once I was firmly in that position, I discovered it to be much more demanding than being Mayor or City Councilman.

In June of 2014, while exercising at my local gym, I fainted and fell face forward on a still-running treadmill. After regaining consciousness and then being attended to by friends and gym staff, I phoned Evan to come and pick me up. In my condition it was unsafe for me to drive, and I would have to leave my vehicle at the gym. I theorized that my blackout was due to my having not eaten for several hours, so I asked Evan to take me to get something to eat.

Along the way to one of our favorite dining destinations, Otter's Chicken, we passed by the local county police and fire precinct. Concerned with my health condition, I asked Evan to pull in to the fire station for me to get a quick blood pressure check, and then we could go on to Otter's.

Inside the station, I apprised the firefighters of my fainting spell at the gym. They quickly went to work checking my blood pressure. The attending firefighter was shocked at how high my reading was. He then began to check my pulse. My heart was beating at over one-hundred forty beats per minute and in an irregular manner. Once again, it appeared that I was experiencing atrial fibrillation.

The firefighters quickly radioed for an ambulance, and several minutes later, I was on my way to Cobb Hospital. Evan would follow the ambulance and call for Lane to join him at the hospital.

60 CENTS

After several hours in the emergency room, and after imploring Evan and Lane to go home and get some sleep, I was transported by ambulance from Cobb Hospital to Piedmont Hospital in Atlanta. There, my team of cardiologists and electrophysiologists who had been overseeing my care during and after my prior atrial fibrillation episodes could diagnose my issues and continue or increase the care and treatment I had been receiving.

I would spend three days as an inpatient at Piedmont. Blood thinners and antiarrhythmic medications were administered to me intravenously. My heart continued in atrial fibrillation. My electrophysiologist, a cardiologist who specializes in the heart's timing, electrical system and on diagnosing and treating irregular heartbeats, suggested that the best resolution for my atrial fibrillation would be to cardiovert my heart.

This procedure involved me being placed under brief sedation while he "shocked" my heart, with the ultimate goal being that my heart would convert to normal sinus rhythm. The cardioversion was successful, and I was allowed to go home the next day.

Going home to my four-thousand square foot house after spending time in the hospital was a daunting task. Experiencing it virtually all alone became depressing and dispiriting. Still on summer break from the University of Georgia, Lane remained living with me at our house. She did her best to make sure I was comfortable. Still, I wanted her to enjoy her vacation time with her friends and didn't want my situation and despair to deter her from leading as normal a life as she could. I would urge Lane to resume her normal activities and not to concern herself with my well-being. I was glad that she did, but I felt alone.

Returning to routine everyday life, I knew that I wasn't alright. My heart was beating normally, but it was feeling lonely. I longed for hope and companionship in my personal life. I deplored going in to work every day at City Hall. Constantly working under a microscope just wasn't my cup of tea.

I wanted to experience happiness. I needed a diversion. It was up to me to change my course in life, with God's help. I prayed daily for peace, joy, and, if it was God's will, a woman who would love me unconditionally and, in turn, I could love her with all my heart. I had no presumption that this would ever occur.

Tracy Sirmans, a representative for the city's engineering firm, had been involved in several projects at the city. Her expertise in event planning and marketing was helpful as we coordinated the opening of the city's new cultural arts center. Additionally, Tracy was involved in several construction projects that were overseen by the engineering firm throughout the city. She was skillful, knowledgeable and attentive to the needs and desires of the city.

I enjoyed working with Tracy and gained tremendous respect for her and for the manner in which she represented herself and the engineering firm. Our relationship was purely professional in nature. That would soon change. After getting up the nerve, I asked Tracy out on a date. After a few days of thought and reflection, she accepted my invitation.

We found that we had a lot in common. We had both been through unsuccessful marriages. Each of us had a heart for our community and for volunteerism and helping those in need. We both loved our families deeply. Tracy didn't have children of her own, but she was someone I felt comfortable having around my kids. I knew that she was an answer to my prayers.

It didn't take long for Tracy and me to discover that we were right for each other. Tracy's soft, quiet voice and her sweet and unassuming manner balanced my outgoing, gregarious and sometimes boisterous personality. Many of our individual interests aligned with each other's. Her father and mother, Jim and Jane Sirmans, were easy to get to know and made me feel welcome in their home. Tracy and I were kindred spirits.

Besides her achievements in business, Tracy has volunteered her gifts of time, talents, energy, and personal resources with such organizations as the American Cancer Society, the YWCA of Northwest Georgia, and the Strand Theater, just to name a few. We believed that God had placed each of us in one another's lives, and our love and respect for one another began to intensify.

Yet another health-related episode of mine left me with no doubt that Tracy truly loved and cared for me, and that it was God's will for us to spend our lives together. At the end of August 2014 and on into September, just over a month after Tracy and I began our relationship, I was experiencing shortness of breath and weakness throughout my body. It was nearly impossible for me to climb a flight of stairs without having to stop to catch my breath. I found it very hard to sleep at night. I coughed incessantly.

A visit to my primary care physician's assistant brought me a diagnosis of pneumonia. He prescribed an antibiotic, an inhaler, and for me to drink plenty of fluids. I did as he instructed, but my condition only worsened. After three days of continual declining health, Tracy insisted that I go back to see my regular physician. She would take me to his office at Atlantic Station in Atlanta, near Piedmont Hospital.

After being called back into an examining room, my primary care physician came in. Knowing me well and my past history with atrial fibrillation, my physician looked at me and could tell immediately that my condition was bad. Putting his hand on my shoulder, and with a caring smile on his face he looked at me and said, "My friend, you need to get over to the emergency room at Piedmont immediately. I will call and let them know you are on the way."

Tracy helped me into her car and drove the short distance to Piedmont Hospital. Arriving in the emergency room, the nurses expeditiously performed an EKG and determined that I was, once again, in atrial fibrillation. An x-ray revealed that my heart was enlarged, and there appeared to be an extraordinary amount of fluid around my heart (probably from the gallons of lemonade I had consumed over the past three days at the physician assistant's orders to intake fluids). They moved me to the cardiac floor of the hospital where the on-call cardiologist ordered a dosage of amiodarone, an anti-arrhythmic drug, to be administered to me in a rapid, high dosage called "bolus".

Once the amiodarone began to enter into my system, I began to lose my ability to breathe and started sweating profusely. As my condition worsened, the cardiologist ordered the nurses to move me to the Cardiac Care Unit (CCU) of the hospital for more intensive care and treatment. As I gasped for air, I felt as if I was going to die. Tracy was by my side throughout it all and up to the point when they got me into the CCU. There, she was escorted to a waiting room while the CCU staff attended to my situation.

After several grueling hours of fighting for my life, the remarkable CCU staff was able to get my breathing back to normal. Tracy was allowed into the room to be with me. When the cardiologist reentered the room with an updated report, the diagnosis wasn't just atrial fibrillation this time. I was also suffering from congestive heart failure.

All of this at the relatively young age of 52. I would spend three nights in CCU. All the while, Tracy was right by my side.

I had never felt as important to someone, and Tracy's expressions of love and care filled my weakened heart as I made every effort to get better. I had found my soulmate, and I loved her deeply. Tracy's family was a source of support and care for her as she cared for my needs. I would soon come to know and love each of them. Evan, Lane and Joseph got to know Tracy's character during my illness. Through her care for me, they were able to accept her as someone special who loved their father.

Tracy and I were married on Saturday, November 29, 2014 in a small ceremony at The Event Station in Powder Springs. Our dear friend, the Reverend Cindy Blocksidge, officiated at our wedding. Both our families were there to share in the special occasion, with the exception of Momma. She was still in the nursing home and in no shape to be present at the wedding. I asked Aunt Dossie to be my surrogate mother for the evening. Momma was with us in spirit, but it was comforting for me to have my dear aunt to stand in for my mother that evening.

Only eight days before our wedding, I had left my position as city manager. I needed to take time to heal and, most importantly, to relieve myself from the stress and strain I had been experiencing in that position. I had learned through this latest health scare that removing negative influences from one's life is important to maintain a quality, balanced life. It was time for me to move on.

Tracy and I would live in my house in Powder Springs. I took the down time I had to concentrate on writing, rekindling my insurance business, and to restore myself back to a new-normal way of living after my recent physical woes. Tracy would return to her position at the engineering firm where she was working, along with continuing her service in various volunteer positions.

There were times when I was alone at home that I would think on my life and all that had taken place. I would recall my childhood days, my first time meeting Joseph, the births of Evan and Lane and the fun times I had experienced with the three of them over the years, our trips to the Czech Republic, my years of community service, my family and friends whom I loved dearly, and my great fortune in having Tracy as my wife and companion.

At times, my thoughts would turn to my Hulsey grandfathers, of how I never got to know either of them, and how they had caused so much pain, suffering and sorrow through their horrific actions and their eventual deaths in the electric chair. I would ponder how the lives of the murder victim's families, and of Daddy, Maw Maw Vert, Aunt Hope and Great-Grandmother Hulsey were significantly impacted and changed forever.

My mind would also wander to Momma and of days gone by when she was in the prime of her life and doing all she could do to provide for our family. When I could muster up the strength, I would take time out of my convalescence to visit her at the nursing home. It was so nice seeing her, to hold her hand, to tell her all about my personal situation, and to share my deep and abiding love and appreciation for her. I knew she couldn't comprehend what I was saying, but it made me feel better just by talking to her.

From time to time, Tracy would join me on my visits to see Momma. Momma would stare and look delightedly into

Tracy's eyes. Somehow, I believe she knew that Tracy was taking good care of her baby boy.

I would frequently find myself thinking about Daddy. There would be many nice thoughts and remembrances along the way. Inevitably, the bitterness I felt toward my father would once again rear its' ugly head as I pondered how and why he had kept the secret of our grandfathers from me up until his death over twenty-seven years ago. I still hadn't rid myself of the anger and frustration I had toward Daddy.

While alone at home one day, I began reveling in my newfound life and how wonderful it had become. I was wrapped up in my own sublimity, oblivious to everything but my own pridefulness. Suddenly, as if he was standing right next to me, I could sense Daddy's presence. It was an eerie sensation that is difficult to describe. I don't believe in ghosts, but I may have encountered one of my own father that particular day. Whatever, or whomever it was, I perceived it was Daddy speaking to me subconsciously.

"Brad, you know that I have always loved you. I know you are upset with me for keeping the secret of your grandfathers from you. There was a good reason for me doing that, Son. For most of my life, I dealt with guilt, hurt and mental anguish for my father's and grandfather's transgressions. I suffered ridicule from people who thought of me as a lowdown, good-for-nothing human simply because of my name and all of the bad that came with it. I spent most of my life living down all of their wrongdoing.

"I know I wasn't as good of a father as you deserved but,

right or wrong, I never had a good example to follow. I'm sorry for that, Son. Aside from loving you, my greatest responsibility to you as your father was to protect you. I know you feel the same for your children. Brad, all I wanted to do was to shield you and Phil from the stigma that had been placed upon me by being the son and grandson of convicted murderers. Now that you know their story, as well as mine, I hope you understand why I never shared the truth about your grandfathers. In the best way I knew how, I was protecting you."

My emotions were all over the map as I began experiencing both sadness and joy at the same time. Sadness came in finally having arrived at the realization that Daddy, acting as a loving and caring father, was protecting Phil and me from the horror and scorn he had dealt with nearly his entire life. I had just spent over half of my life in my own selfish pity not knowing and appreciating the sacrifices Daddy had made for us, so that we could hopefully live a better and happier life from his own.

The joy I felt was that, after fifty-plus years of wondering what made Daddy tick, and why he said and did many of the things he did, I now could fully comprehend and accept the man my father was. He was an awesome and imperfect man who carried a huge weight on his shoulders from his family's history. As far as I was concerned, he was the most courageous man I had ever known. He bore the burdens of our family's past so that Momma, Phil and I could have a better life than his.

While I still harbor some animosity against Daddy over

some of the things he said and did, I can now reconcile his secrecy and sometimes poor behavior with the knowledge that he had lived a difficult, complex life that most people have never had to face. He had lost two siblings as a toddler. He had lost both his father and grandfather at the tender young age of eight in such a traumatic manner. He would move from place to place as his mother and my grandmother, Maw Maw Vert, would struggle to raise Daddy and Aunt Hope during the Great Depression, without Granddaddy's support.

For most of his childhood and teen years, Daddy continued to live and attend school in Rockmart, the same small town where the murders had taken place, and where everyone knew the story of the Hulsey family. According to Momma's account, he was ridiculed and bullied by some of his classmates and certain townspeople for something he had absolutely nothing to do with, except that he shared his father's name, Fred Avery Hulsey, Jr.

Momma said that it was good and caring men in Rockmart like the two "town drunks" that we used to see on weekends drinking seltzer water with a Goody's Powder mixed in at the City Drug Company "fountain," who would take up for Daddy and do their best to protect him. With courage and determination, Daddy continued to live in Rockmart, and he would go on to serve in many capacities within the community and, ultimately, be named to the Rockmart Hall of Fame.

The secret Daddy kept from me had been unveiled nearly three decades before. Finally understanding his motives and his true love for our family brought peace and light to the quandary I had struggled through most of my adult life. I long to hold him one day in Heaven, to tell him how much I love him, and how much I appreciate all he went through so that he could shield us from the shame and sorrow he had lived with most of his life.

With my lovely bride, Tracy

CHAPTER SEVENTEEN: REMEMBRANCE

Having come to terms with Daddy after so many years was, yet, another blessing for me. The relief I felt when I fully discovered and understood Daddy's motives in keeping the story of my grandfathers hidden was comforting. I was able to move on beyond the uncertainty I had about his ability and desire to be a good father.

Daddy felt it was his duty to safeguard us against any dishonor and harm that might come our way as a result of our ancestry. In doing so, he kept Phil and me from having to bear the burdens he had shouldered for most of his life. I was now able to see Daddy as a loving and caring father.

My love and gratitude for Daddy is immeasurable. I never really felt close to him when he was alive, but I was now experiencing the special bond of a father and son. I wanted Daddy to be proud of me. I hope he is, and I hope one day to have him tell me so. I long to hold my father, and to share and receive genuine and unabated love.

I was fortunate to still have one of my parents alive to love and care for, albeit a less than desirable lifestyle for her to live, or for those of us who loved her to witness. Now eighty-eight-years-old, Momma's physical and mental state had declined significantly. The nursing home provided exceptional care for her, but the quality of life she had enjoyed for most of her life had now dissipated.

60 CENTS

Momma could no longer talk, feed, dress or bathe herself. She was incontinent, and her teeth were rotting due to the inability of her and her caretakers to brush her teeth. All any of us could do would be to keep her comfortable and to love on her as much as possible.

For over five years, Momma had spent her days in a wheelchair, scratching her head, grinding what teeth she had left, smiling sometimes and frowning others. She appeared to be in a faraway place, detached from her surroundings.

Phil would come from Tennessee to see Momma as often as he could. He would never question the methods of care I would decide upon for her. I had his unequivocal support as I determined what I felt was in Momma's best interests. Aunt Dossie would visit as often as one of her girls was able to bring her from Rockmart.

On May 17, 2015, as I was making one of my routine visits to check in on Momma, there was a noticeable change in her countenance. She was lethargic, her body limp and her head slouched over.

She seemed almost comatose as I called her name. I couldn't garner the usual smile and acknowledgement when I would call to her, "Momma? Momma? Look at me – it's Brad." Her time here on earth was drawing to a close. The nursing home physician called for hospice care to come in and attend to Momma's final dying needs.

The next day, Momma would be placed into her bed for the

last time. For two days, lying semi-comatose, she remained unresponsive. Our dear friend and pastor, Cindy Blocksidge, who had performed Tracy's and my wedding ceremony back in November of 2014, came to visit Momma on May 19th. As she lay in her bed in a lifeless state, Cindy lovingly rubbed Momma's hand as if she had known her for years. She spoke to her as if she was listening. Perhaps she was.

Cindy told Momma that she had lived a good, long life, and that it was okay for her to go on and be with God and all of her loved ones in Heaven. All of her living family members were doing fine, and she needn't feel as if she had to stick around for any reason. Continually stroking her hand, Cindy then read Psalm 23, "Yea, though I walk through the valley of the shadow of death, I will fear no evil: for thou art with me; thy rod and thy staff they comfort me," and then, "Surely goodness and mercy will follow me all the days of my life: and I will dwell in the house of the Lord forever."

I don't know if Cindy's visit was meant to ease Momma in her last days, but I can assure anyone that it gave me an inner peace and a feeling of comfort as I watched Momma respire some of her last breaths. I was grateful to Cindy for giving of her time to be with Momma and for her passion of serving and caring for others.

Alone with Momma after Cindy's visit, I spoke to her as a little child, clinging to her as I offered my love and adoration for her, both audibly and by tenderly laying my head against hers. I reminisced about days gone by and about the loving, memorable times we as a family had shared throughout the years. I whispered to her that I would see her tomorrow, and that it was alright if she felt she needed to go on to be with Daddy and the rest of her family and friends.

I kissed Momma's cheek one last time as I left with tears of sadness streaming down my eyes. I really didn't want to leave her. I felt in my heart of hearts that this would be the last time I would see her alive. I was right.

The next morning, only minutes after Tracy and I had arisen from our night's rest, I received a call from the hospice nurse. Momma had died early that morning, Wednesday, May 20, 2015. She had fought the good fight and somehow had managed to live and cope with Alzheimer's Disease for nearly nine years. Her body, mind and soul were now at peace in Heaven.

As Tracy held me in her comforting arms, my mind raced back to days gone by, good times, when I knew that I had Momma to share all of my life's experiences in an unconditional, loving atmosphere. I held Tracy tighter, comforted by the knowledge that I now had her to fill the void Momma's passing had left. My heart and mind overflowed with blessed memories of the love and support my dear mother had provided me since my birth. I knew I would truly miss her.

Allowing Phil, Deborah and their family ample time to arrive in town from Tennessee, we would hold Momma's funeral in the chapel of the Freeman Harris Funeral Home on Saturday, May 23rd. Momma was finally back home in

Rockmart. Phil and I would preside at her funeral, in accordance with Momma's wishes to, "Not have a bunch of preaching at my funeral." We would bury her at the Rockmart Memorial Gardens, next to Daddy, who had passed away twenty-eight years earlier.

Next to their burial site are the graves of Momma's parents and my maternal grandparents, Poppy and Maw Maw Holland, as well as her brother and my uncle, Lum Holland. Their physical bodies were now forever entombed nearby one another as their heavenly bodies were enjoying each other's company in the presence of God. It was a sad day, but knowing that Momma was no longer suffering made it a day of rejoicing, too. The one person who had made the greatest profound impact on my life was now gone.

I thought to myself – the mother that had inspired me for all of my life had actually left many years ago due to the scourge of Alzheimer's. I would vow to remember her in the same context of the words from the book and movie *Brian's Song* that had been spoken at Daddy's funeral in 1987 – "When I remember Momma, it's not how she died that I will remember but, how she lived. How she did live!"

Martha Holland Hulsey (Momma)

CHAPTER EIGHTEEN: RETROSPECTION

Momma's death gave me pause to ruminate not only on her life, but on my own, as well. I have a beautiful, loving and caring wife in Tracy. Joseph, Evan and Lane are making me proud every day through their goodness and personal achievements. My business is continuing to build as I concentrate my efforts on growth and success. My health is improving daily as my heart grows stronger, allowing me to discontinue taking many of my medications. My relationship with God is closer than ever as He guides my paths in all of my life situations.

As I look back, I see that I was robbed of a close relationship with Daddy by my grandfathers' actions. Spending his whole life living down the wicked and wretched deeds of his father and grandfather left Daddy little time or energy to focus his love and attention toward Momma, Phil and me. Their murderous rampage, incarceration, trial and executions scarred my father his entire life.

Daddy's tireless community service was no doubt inspired by his desire to be a better person than his father, and to overcome the stigma that had been placed upon him as he continued living in Rockmart. Inevitably, I believe that Daddy's drinking problems toward the end of his life were due not only to his declining health, but also to his need to escape the emotional and mental anguish he had experienced due to my grandfathers' transgressions and eventual fate in Georgia's electric chair.

It is clear to me now why Senator Richard B. Russell wished to appoint Daddy to the U.S. Military Academy at West Point, New York back in 1942. As governor, Russell had stayed my grandfathers' executions on several occasions. In the end, it was he who had the final say-so on carrying out the death sentences imposed upon them.

I want to believe that someone as staunch and unabashed in his personal and political convictions as Senator Russell ultimately had a caring heart. Russell wanted Daddy to attend the Academy to atone for his having to issue the final order of execution of Daddy's father and grandfather.

****

All humans are uniquely made and, therefore, we see, hear, feel, touch and smell things through our senses in a different manner sometimes. Not long ago, I asked Phil to share with me his feelings and emotions regarding our upbringing and how Daddy, our family, and the community had kept the secret from us for so long.

"It kind of upsets me that both sides of our family kept all of this secret. How much did they know and why wouldn't they let us in on some of it so that we could know what Daddy was going through? It also upsets me that Momma never talked to me about 'the story'. No one in Rockmart has ever shared any of this with me. I sense that Daddy did everything he thought was right to protect us."

It is interesting to note the unambiguous fact that I had held Daddy totally responsible for keeping the secret for so long from Phil and me. Conversely, Phil places the blame on Momma and our entire family. Growing up as children, and even on into our adult lives, Phil and I both felt like he was always Daddy's "favorite" son, and that I was Momma's. Perhaps this is exhibited in how each of us perceived the cover-up of our family's secret.

My anger and frustration had been centered on Daddy for several years. It continued up until that unexpected, revealing moment when I sensed Daddy explaining himself to me and, then, my subsequent epiphany as to why he had kept the secret from me. I hope and pray that one day my dear brother Phil attains the closure I have found. I wish I could give it to him.

Evan, Lane and Joseph rarely speak of our grandfathers. Like me, they never knew them or got to meet them. Sadly, they never got to meet Daddy, nor did two of Phil and Deborah's children, Sarah and Blake. For the first four years of his life Phil's oldest son, Mitch, would be the only grandchild out of six that ever was acquainted with Daddy. Daddy and Mitch grew to be best buddies, and Daddy was so proud to have a grandson to hang out with. I know Daddy would have loved the other grandchildren and would be so proud of them, too. Neither Phil nor I have never pressured either of the children to learn more about the criminal actions of our grandfathers.

Naturally, not possessing the Hulsey DNA makes Joseph less desirous of wanting to know more about the story.

That's okay. Lane has never been overly curious about our family beyond Momma's and Daddy's generation. At times, she exhibits some enthusiasm in the story surrounding our grandfathers' plight. Not a problem, either. Contrastingly, Evan has shown more interest than the other two children, taking time to listen to my stories of my discoveries, and asking questions about the facts surrounding our Hulsey family's story.

One afternoon, Evan, Lane and I traveled to Rockmart on a very specialized mission. I had discovered where the abandoned well was located that Granddaddy and Great-Granddaddy Hulsey had dumped the three bodies of Cliff Jones, Lige Harper and Ernest McCullough in. I wanted to use all of my senses to soak up the surroundings where my grandfathers had walked in a drunken stupor and inhumanely attempted to hide the corpses of their murdered victims. We set out on a journey that day to discover a piece of our Hulsey family history.

The pathway into the woods my grandfathers took with the mule drawn wagon and the bodies in tow no longer existed. The elderly man and woman who owned the property where the well exists said the only direct route to our desired destination was to cross the upper lake above Coots Lake. We borrowed an old, rickety plastic boat from them and paddled our way toward the land area where, at some point, the abandoned well was situated.

Arriving at the other side of the lake and exiting the boat, Evan walked alone on one side of what appeared to be a worn and overgrown earthen roadway ridden with fallen pine trees and thick mounds of leaves, while Lane and I walked on the other side. Having traversed the mountainous landscape for only a few minutes, Evan suddenly exclaimed, "Hey, Pops. I think I've found it!"

With Lane following close behind, I approached the area where Evan was standing. Looking down, I peered upon a large opening in the ground that, without a doubt, was the old abandoned well.

This was one of the most surreal moments of my life. I paused to collect my thoughts and to reflect on the occasion. I uttered to the children, "Just think, our grandfathers actually stood in this place many years ago and attempted to cover up the senseless, sinister murders they had committed."

Closing my eyes for a moment, I was transformed back to June 19, 1930. The mystical, emanating aura placed me in the presence of the grey mule and the wagon it drew, of my grandfathers in their drunken and terrified state, and of the three murdered men and their lifeless, mangled, and bloodied bodies entombed in the makeshift grave we stood upon. For that brief moment, my emotions were being pulled and tugged by the awesome power of the scene playing out in my mind.

Before leaving home that day on our mission to the well, I had deeply tucked away six dimes into my pants pocket. I didn't want them to fall loosely out of my pocket, and I hoped to prevent the clanging sound they would have made as they jostled around. For me, the coins held a very personal and sentimental meaning. Waiting for the precise time when Evan and Lane were not looking, I quietly hurled the dimes into the abandoned well and then, using my hands, swept leaves on top to cover them from anyone's sight.

There, interred with the memories of what had taken place so many years ago, I symbolically paid personal homage with my own 60 cents. One dime each in sympathy and remembrance of Cliff Jones, Lige Harper, and Ernest McCullough; and one each for Granddaddy and Great-Granddaddy Hulsey, with my sincerest hope that they had confessed their sins and had asked for forgiveness before their executions.

The sixth dime was emblematic of my love, respect and admiration for Daddy. He had sacrificed and endured so much for our family. It was time for me to bury the past hurts and anger I had felt toward him, knowing that he had loved me enough to protect me from the evil brought to pass by my grandfathers' iniquities.

The abandoned well was a place I had wanted to visit, and I was glad to have had Evan and Lane along to share the experience with me. Nevertheless, in that quiet and serene wooded landscape, all I could feel was sadness, disgust and remorse for what had taken place there eighty-four years prior.

As the kids and I departed, I was overcome with emotion in knowing all that had transpired in that solemn place, and in having stood in the same place that my grandfathers had on that fateful night in 1930. I thought of my friend Lavay McCullough, and how he had lost his father at the age of one-year-old. I recalled that it had only been a matter of a few months since Lavay had offered redemptive grace to me for the guilt I felt for my grandfathers' offenses. I longed to see him again in the future.

****

I would have the opportunity to, once again, meet with Lavay McCullough, in January of 2016. Tracy and I had planned an overnight visit to see Lane in Athens, Georgia, where she was attending the University of Georgia. The following day, we would be heading for an evening's stay in Helen, Georgia, one of our favorite mountain getaways.

Travelling between those two destinations, we would make a stopover to meet Lavay for lunch in Cornelia, Georgia, where he had been living for several years. I had called him and arranged our visit a few days earlier.

It had been nearly three years since my luncheon with Lavay and his family at Sidekicks in Rockmart. Tracy and I arrived a few minutes early at the Cornelia Chick Fil-A restaurant where we would be meeting him. Looking with anticipation out of the rain-soaked front window, my eye caught a glimpse of a man walking with a cane. It was Lavay. I was overjoyed as I greeted him at the door of the restaurant.

After introducing Tracy and Lavay to one another, I invited him to join us as our guest for lunch. Tracy volunteered to place our orders as Lavay and I began to reminisce on our prior visits. I asked him how he had been feeling, and Lavay indicated that he was doing well, except that he was dealing with an affliction known as "post-polio syndrome".

This condition affects 25% to 50% of the people who have previously survived poliomyelitis and typically occurs several years after the infection has been brought under control. It had affected Lavay's ability to walk upright, but it hadn't taken away his independence or his tenacity for life.

At my request, just as he had during our visit together in Rockmart, Lavay had brought along the only photo he has of his father, Ernest McCullough. He also had with him a book that his son, Andy, had compiled for his mother and father on the occasion of their 50th wedding anniversary back in 2008.

As Tracy perused the anniversary book, I gazed at the photo of Ernest McCullough, hoping to feel his presence in some sort of way as his son and I spoke with one another. I could see the resemblance of Lavay to his father as my eyes would move from the photo to the face of the wonderful man sitting in front of me.

I asked Lavay if it was okay for me to interrogate him about his life and about his knowledge of the events surrounding his father's murder. He gladly offered any answers he could provide.

I asked him what he knew about his father. Just as he had

indicated during our visit in Rockmart in 2013, Lavay offered, "He was a good poker player. He had a special way of shuffling the deck of cards that amazed a lot of people." Beyond that, he didn't, or perhaps couldn't, offer any more insight into his knowledge of his father.

I queried Lavay about his father's murder, wondering what he knew about the circumstances surrounding it. "My father, your grandfathers and the other men were there at your grandfather's farm, drinking and gambling. Evidently, my father and the other fellows were winning quite handily, so your grandfathers shot them dead. My Uncle Doyle once told me that my father raised his hands above his face to hopefully stop the bullets."

All of the evidence I had found in news stories and court documents indicates that each of the three men, including Lavay's father, had been shot in the back of their heads. I shared this with him, and he seemed surprised by the news.

Lavay went on to share what, for him, was the most important story he had learned about his father. "My grandmother, my mother's mother, once shared with me that before the day my father was killed, she had spoken to him about the Lord, and about the good news that Jesus had died for his sins. She witnessed to him about God's grace, eternal life in Heaven, and forgiveness of sins. I don't know if my father accepted the Lord as his personal Savior or not."

Beyond what he had conveyed to me regarding his father's murder and all the before and after related to it, Lavay didn't know much more. It struck me how Daddy's and Lavay's generation, commonly referred to as the "Greatest Generation," made up of persons born from 1901 to 1945, differed in many ways from the "Baby Boomers" generation I am a member of, compiled of persons born between 1946 and 1965.

Most revealing to me is how my generation has a need to know all of the details about any situation and is willing to talk about virtually anything. Not only did I have a burning desire to learn all I could about my family's secret, I can also recall Lavay's children's interest in the story as I told it that day in April 2013.

Contrarily, Daddy's and Lavay's generation are reticent with specifics surrounding family affairs and graphic accounts of gruesome activities. For reasons I now understand, Daddy never shared the tale of my grandfathers' crimes and executions with me. As I sat and listened intently to him, I discovered that Lavay hadn't learned much over the years about his father's life and subsequent murder at the hands of Granddaddy and Great-Granddaddy Hulsey.

Lavay said that, after his father's death, his mother was in a "fog" for many years. He reminded me that his mother was unable to care for him and that he had moved to Porterdale to live with his grandmother who would provide him with love and support for many years.

Lavay eventually returned to Rockmart and lived happily with his mother, Louise and her new husband, J.B. Lee.

After attending and graduating from Rockmart High School, he left home to attend Oxford College of Emory University in Oxford, Georgia. A few years later he went on to receive his Bachelor of Liberal Arts degree from Mercer University in Macon, Georgia. Afterward, Lavay and his wife, Gladys, with their daughter Belinda in tow, left Georgia for Fort Worth, Texas. There, after three years of study, Lavay received a Masters of Theology degree from Southwestern Baptist Theological Seminary.

Throughout his years of education and for many decades to come, Lavay would serve various Baptist churches as Pastor, having brought many people to belief in Jesus Christ as their Lord and Savior. He continues to serve God in his local church and beyond.

Another story Lavay told me during our visit that day had to do with Daddy, one that I had never heard before. Having returned to live with his mother and stepfather in Rockmart, Lavay became involved in the local Boy Scouts of America troop. He enjoyed the various activities that helped him to grow as a young man and to receive recognition for hard work and determination. The Boy Scouts gave him an opportunity to hone his skills in many areas and to serve in the community.

Lavay went on to share that Daddy had served as his Assistant Scoutmaster during his time in the local Boy Scout troop. He said that Daddy would assist him and the other Scouts with their various activities and in earning their merit badges.

60 CENTS

I was amazed by the story of how Daddy had mentored Lavay and helped him become a better Boy Scout by offering his time and expertise. They were able to move beyond their family's atrocious historical connection to form their own positive relationship. This warmed my heart deeply.

After having talked for more than three hours, the time had come for Tracy and me to depart and continue on our trip to Helen. Before saying our goodbyes to Lavay, I had one last question of him. Back on September 29, 2015, I had seen photos of Lavay's mother, Louise, posted by his son Andy on his Facebook page.

Along with the photos, Andy posted this message, "Today is my Grandma Louise's birthday. She would have been 109 (and she would have been very upset that I just told the world that). I loved her and still do. She was a great lady. She never finished high school because she needed to work to help support her family.

"She went through a lot of hardships - most trying of which was being a young widow during the Depression with a son who had polio - and never complained. She always put others before herself. She loved to laugh and was quick to serve. When I was about my boys' ages I didn't like that she always wanted to kiss me when she saw me but I would welcome that now."

I told Lavay how I had enjoyed seeing the photos of his mother, including one of him in his mother's arms when he was just a tiny boy. My parting question to Lavay was,

"How old was your mother when she passed away?" Lavay thought for a moment and replied, "My mother was ninety-six years old when she died. All in all, she lived a good, long life."

I thought, how wonderful it is that Lavay's mother had lived such a long, meaningful life. She overcame the hardships she had endured as a young widow all alone and "in a fog" as Lavay had so aptly termed her condition after the death of her husband, Ernest.

Similarly, Maw Maw Vert, who had sustained a tremendous amount of heartbreak and struggles throughout her life, lived to be ninety-five years old. Both of these remarkable women had experienced many trials and tribulations along their lives' odyssey, and were able to persevere in spite of their many obstacles.

Helping him into his car, and not knowing when I might see him again, I wanted to share a final thought with Lavay. Thinking of all that he had gone through in his life, and how he was such a good, decent and accomplished man, I said to him, "I know that if he had lived long enough to have seen you grow into the man you are, your father would be very proud of you."

With a warm smile and a gratified nod of his head, Lavay drove away. It had been another blessed, uplifting experience having been in his presence.

Lane and Evan at the well

Lavay McCullough, holding a photo of his father, Ernest McCullough

CHAPTER NINETEEN: REFLECTION

I have had many years to reflect on the story of my grandfathers, and how the circumstances surrounding it have impacted and changed the lives of so many people. The McCullough, Jones and Harper families lost their loved ones through Granddaddy's and Great-Granddaddy's savage acts. Maw Maw Vert lost her husband, and Daddy and Aunt Hope lost their father and grandfather.

Just like with Phil and me, our first cousins and Aunt Hope's children, Diana, Jeff, Don and Julia, would never meet our Granddaddy Hulsey. For most of their lives they were unaware of the circumstances surrounding Grand-daddy's death at such an early age. Aunt Hope and Uncle J.R. had kept the family secret from them, as well, undoubtedly to protect them just like Daddy had done for Phil and me.

As Phil articulated, neither side of our family nor anyone in Rockmart had ever told us the story of our grandfathers. It is truly amazing that it could be kept so quiet. I know that our family held the secret tightly because that is what Daddy wanted. They loved him and, commendably, re-spected and honored his wishes.

In spite of the shame and degradation my grandfathers' criminal actions brought to the community, the greater majority of the citizens of Rockmart loved and cared for our family, without reservation or hesitation. I count it a great honor and privilege to have grown up in such a wonderful hometown.

My life by no means has been perfect. After all, who among us has had such a life? Right now, mine is as good as I have ever had, and I feel like a truly blessed man.

There are those good days when all seems right with the world and nothing can go wrong. Occasionally, there are those bad days, when sorrow, darkness, anger, frustration or temptation creep into my soul and create an unpleasant environment.

In between the good and bad days are the most common of all – regular, neutral days, characterized by normalcy and basic, ordinary living. My life has truly been a "rollercoaster," with its' ups and downs, as well as some steadiness of its' course. The difference between a rollercoaster and life, however, is stark. You can get off of a rollercoaster if you want, but you can't get off of life. Life continues on and on, up, down and steady. I'll gladly take that ride anytime.

In the end, we all have one life to live, one death to give, and one day of final judgement to face. In some shape, form or fashion we all have our own "60 cents" to spare at the end of our lives. Hopefully, we will have lived full and meaningful lives, defined by our love for God, our family, and our fellow man, and for leaving this world a little bit better off than when we arrived upon it.

It was an unforgettable experience delving into my family's

history and reliving my own life up to now. I believe that, in order to know yourself, you must understand your heritage and your past. My chance meeting in 1987 with Lavay McCullough, the eventual disclosure of the secret that had been held so close from me, and the revealing details that I have been able to uncover have given me a greater understanding of who I am and where I came from.

As I continue along my life's journey, I still sometimes find it difficult to abide comfortably in it. For if a story of such great magnitude could be kept from me for such a long time, I have to pause and wonder – what other secrets lie in waiting that I have yet to discover?

With my friend and one of the finest men I've ever known,
Lavay McCullough

CPSIA information can be obtained
at www.ICGtesting.com
Printed in the USA
LVOW01s0202061016
507480LV00001B/4/P